D0535240

PERENNIALS

FACING PAGE

Apiaceae
Eryngium amethystinum
(x 1.75)

EVERGREEN is an imprint of Benedikt Taschen Verlag GmbH

© for this edition: 1999 Benedikt Taschen Verlag GmbH
Hohenzollernring 53, D–50672 Köln
© 1998 Editions du Chêne – Hachette Livre – Plantes Vivaces
Under the direction of Paul Starosta
Text: Marion Ferraud
Photographs: Paul Starosta
Text editor: Cécile Aoustin
Layout: Christopher Evans
Translation: Anthea Bell in association with First Edition Translations Ltd, Cambridge
Realization of the English edition by First Edition Translations Ltd, Cambridge

Printed in Italy
ISBN 3–8228–6514–1

PERENNIALS

Photographs PAUL STAROSTA
Text MARION FERRAUD

EVERGREEN

Contents

The world of perennials
6

ASTERACEAE
16

LAMIACEAE
32

LILIACEAE
42

MALVACEAE
48

PAPAVERACEAE
52

OENOTHERACEAE
58

RANUNCULACEAE
62

SAXIFRAGACEAE
74

SOLANACEAE
80

OTHER GENERA AND SPECIES
86

Practical guide
116

GLOSSARY
126

INDEX
127

BIBLIOGRAPHY
128

USEFUL ADDRESSES
128

The world of perennials

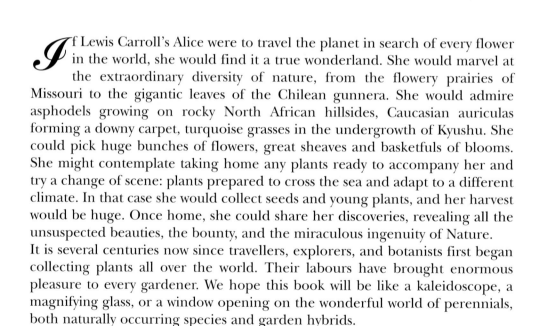

*I*f Lewis Carroll's Alice were to travel the planet in search of every flower in the world, she would find it a true wonderland. She would marvel at the extraordinary diversity of nature, from the flowery prairies of Missouri to the gigantic leaves of the Chilean gunnera. She would admire asphodels growing on rocky North African hillsides, Caucasian auriculas forming a downy carpet, turquoise grasses in the undergrowth of Kyushu. She could pick huge bunches of flowers, great sheaves and basketfuls of blooms. She might contemplate taking home any plants ready to accompany her and try a change of scene: plants prepared to cross the sea and adapt to a different climate. In that case she would collect seeds and young plants, and her harvest would be huge. Once home, she could share her discoveries, revealing all the unsuspected beauties, the bounty, and the miraculous ingenuity of Nature.

It is several centuries now since travellers, explorers, and botanists first began collecting plants all over the world. Their labours have brought enormous pleasure to every gardener. We hope this book will be like a kaleidoscope, a magnifying glass, or a window opening on the wonderful world of perennials, both naturally occurring species and garden hybrids.

Dipsacaceae
Scabiosa caucasica
(x 1)

The term 'perennial' came into use among English gardeners and landscape designers at the end of the nineteenth century. They coined it as the most appropriate name for a large group of plants originally native to very different areas, but sharing the ability to survive for more than two seasons in a moderate climate. 'Perennial' is the term for plants that can be left in the open ground and will tolerate winter frosts, coming up again year after year. It is chiefly applied to herbaceous* plants. Strictly speaking, trees and woody shrubs are perennials too, but they are not usually listed under that heading. However, the group does include certain rhizomatous* plants (irises), bulbous plants (crocosmia, Kaffir lily), small shrubs (helianthemum, lavender) and biennials that seed themselves easily (foxglove).

The names of perennials

All plants have Latin botanical names. Take *Centaurea montana* as an example: the first name, *Centaurea*, is the name of the genus; the second, *montana*, is the name of the species. The species name is often descriptive. Alternatively, it may refer to the plant's original habitat or the person who discovered it. *Centaurea montana*, for instance, is mountain knapweed, *Lavandula angustifolia* is narrow-leaved lavender, *Verbena bonariensis* is verbena of Buenos Aires, *Phlox douglasii* is a phlox brought back to Europe by David Douglas.

When a plant has been created by selection or hybridisation, its genus and species names are followed by a variety name. Variety names are often given in the plant breeder's own language, and may refer to the plant's appearance, for instance *Pulsatilla vulgaris* 'Rubra' and *Saxifraga aizoon* 'Minor', or to the breeder, or someone to whom the breeder wants to pay a special compliment, as with *Paeonia lactiflora* 'Sarah Bernhardt'. It may also refer to a place, most often the place where the plant was bred, for instance *Heuchera* 'Bressingham'.

Scrophulariaceae
Digitalis purpurea hybrid
(x 1)

FOLLOWING PAGE

Scrophulariaceae
Mimulus aurantiacus
(x 2)

A LOVE AFFAIR WITH PERENNIALS

Those lucky enough to acquire a plot of land for a garden usually begin by sowing annuals* near the house, and their abundance of flowers will provide instant gratification. But then new garden owners may perhaps come upon a bed of yellow achilleas and day lilies flourishing in some corner where they were planted by a previous, green-fingered occupant of the property. They admire the campanulas cascading over the dry-stone wall next door. As they begin to appreciate the hardy* plants which flower regularly and vigorously every year, establishing themselves quite naturally in the garden, it occurs to them to grow perennials instead of annuals that need to be replaced every spring, or alternatively overwintered under cover, not an easy task. Taking their curiosity a little further and consulting a few books on

the subject, they will soon realise what riches Nature has placed at their disposal.

Easy, hardy, and rewarding

New gardeners often start by planting some species suggested by a helpful neighbour. While they are still novices, they may begin with attractive plants that flower over a long period and are easily divided, such as Michaelmas daisies, rudbeckias and gaillardias. They may sow the seed of plants like hollyhocks, evening primroses, and perhaps gauras where they are to flower. Soon they will find themselves perusing catalogues and visiting specialist nurseries to look for more unusual plants.

Flowers for all seasons, plants for all situations

The gardener will discover that there are interesting perennials for every season of the year, and the garden is the scene of constant change, with different flowers blooming in succession from spring to winter. And there is more to them than just their flowers: their shapes and foliage are further attractive features. An architectural plant like *Artemisia* 'Powis Castle' or *Miscanthus sinensis* at the back of a border gives structure to its entire composition; variegated ground-cover plants such as *Lamiastrum galeobdolon* 'Variegatum' will lighten the heavy shade of a chestnut tree. Finally, with their enormous diversity, perennials can provide something to suit every situation: damp soil, poor soil, a dry slope, shade, full sun. There are very few parts of the garden that cannot be successfully colonised by well-chosen perennials.

Pleasure and a sense of adventure

The gardener will grow more and more enthusiastic as the original plot becomes the scene of creative development. You need not be a professional landscape gardener to design your own world of plants, and another very attractive aspect of perennials is that they are very easy to propagate. As you sow seed, divide rootstocks and separate offsets, you acquire a whole stock of new plants to be put in round the original parent or anywhere else you like.

An invitation to travel

While some perennials immediately transport us back to the gardens of our childhood, others evoke the atmosphere of distant lands. The geographical, climatic and ecological origin of a plant is a fascinating subject to the enquiring mind. Knowing that the graceful avens (*Geum chiloense*) flowers naturally in the Chilean prairies, or that *Macleaya cordata* flourishes in the fields of Taiwan and China, adds to the pleasure of growing these plants in our own gardens. It is amusing to discover that by a fortunate coincidence *Salvia uliginosa* and *Verbena bonariensis*, one of Brazilian and the other of Argentinian origin, grow well side by side. As you look at the little Labrador violet, very much at home in European gardens, where it will seed freely, it is quite hard to remember that it comes from Canada. How many of us know that the agapanthus, kniphofia, phygelius (Cape fuchsia), crocosmia, galtonia and diascia are all natives of South Africa, so that they are likely to thrive in similar conditions? And a glance at Asiatic plants will soon show that the undergrowth of China, Japan and Korea has given us many plants suitable for cool or shady gardens; they include anemone, bergenia, ophiopogon, liriope, pachysandra, rheum, hosta and houttuynia.

Caryophyllaceae
Dianthus arenarius
(x 3)

Polemoniaceae
Phlox paniculata
(x 0.5)

Adapting to survive unfavourable conditions

The outstanding characteristic of perennials is their enormous diversity. Think of the contrast between a little androsace tucked in between a couple of stones, and a vigorous delphinium brightening a large area of the garden. The charm of these plants lies in such contrasts, and the contrasts arise from the extraordinary variety and wealth of their natural habitats. Studying the botany of a plant helps us to understand how it adapted to its original habitat in order to resist summer droughts, waterlogged ground, windy or cold conditions. Perennials have undergone some very varied morphological adaptations to help them survive the winter.

Storage organs

In the majority of species, of course, the storage organs are roots, which may or may not be swollen to a greater or lesser extent. The aquilegia has a swollen rootstock, the liatris a tuberous* root, and the dicentra and the peony also have swollen roots. Reserves may also be stored in rhizomes, elongated underground stems; rhizomatous plants include irises and Solomon's seal. Bulbs such as those of the crocosmia are also short, tuberous underground stems. Finally, certain succulents like sedums may have storage organs above the ground.

Buds in waiting

Another characteristic of perennials is the presence of *dormant buds*. If the top-growth of a plant dies back in winter, the new vegetation develops from these buds in spring. Their actual location on the plant varies. It may be:
– in direct contact with the soil in many ground-cover perennials, including cushion-forming plants (armeria, pink), rosette-forming plants (androsace, saxifrage) and mat-forming plants (lysimachia, sedum);
– on or just below the surface of the soil, as in Michaelmas daisies, achilleas and *Phlox paniculata*. The dormant buds of rhizomatous plants (iris) and tuberous plants (peony, dicentra) are also situated here; rhizomes may rot if they are planted too deep. But some perennials, including a number of bulbs (lilies and fritillaries), need to have their dormant buds further below ground level;
– on the stems of such evergreen or semi-evergreen* plants as iberis, helianthemum, santolina and periwinkle (*Vinca minor*).

These morphological characteristics are a useful indication of the best way to propagate the plants. You usually need only take those sections of the plant that bear dormant buds and encourage them to put out new roots.

Knowing something about a plant's original home is the best way to understand its likes and dislikes, and helps the gardener to avoid disappointment. For instance, you will realise why there is no point in trying to plant a catananche in a border on heavy clay that is regularly waterlogged in winter once you know that catananche, a Mediterranean plant, likes well-drained soil. Nor is it sensible to plant an astilbe in a south-facing situation, since its natural home is in the humid undergrowth on the mountains of China and Japan.

Though the garden is an artificial landscape made by human beings, the juxtaposition of its little ecosystems still means that certain rules must be respected. The gardener's skill consists of growing a wide range of plant material in harmony with the natural background.

Resistant cells

The tissues are in a state of suspended animation in those parts of the plant that survive the worst of the winter (root system, dormant buds, evergreen stems and foliage). Cold slows down their activity and inhibits growth, but does not kill them.

These tissues consist of cells that are hydrated to a greater or lesser extent and have an extra-cellular liquid in between them. When the weather is freezing, crystals form both inside and outside the cells. Whether the cells are destroyed or not depends on the ability of the cell walls to resist being pushed out of shape by these crystals. If the tissue is dehydrated, the concentration of dissolved bodies in it lowers its freezing point; if colloids* keep the water supercooled* then a drop in temperature has an inhibiting but not necessarily destructive effect. When the temperature falls gradually, crystals form outside the cells, water is drawn out of the cells by osmosis*, and they become dehydrated. The cell walls are deformed, cellular volume diminishes and the concentration of aqueous solutions between the cells increases, preventing the formation of crystals inside the cells. Some tissues are more resistant than others (woody tissue, the dry scales of buds) while tender tissues containing more water (leaves, young stems) are more likely to die.

The importance of climate

Climatic factors are extremely important. Winter damage to plants is the result of the speed with which frost sets in, the length of time it lasts, and the moment in the growth cycle when it begins, as well as the intensity of the frost itself. The surrounding humidity rate is a prime factor: a plant full of water will not stand up to the destructive effects of cold weather as well as a more dehydrated plant. On the other hand, in a prolonged cold period when water is frozen and no longer available to the plant, there is a risk of severe dehydration.

Study of these cellular phenomena helps us to understand the concept of hardiness and make the correct deductions from the conditions in a plant's natural habitat. It may be perennial in its original home and able to resist intense cold because the air there has low humidity, or because it is covered by a protective layer of snow. It will not resist frost so well in a humid climate or on heavy soil. One should never lose sight of the fact that perennials, like all garden plants, are living organisms to be treated with care.

Liliaceae
Asphodelus fistulosa
(x 1)

Up until the early eighteenth century the private garden was chiefly utilitarian, and flowers were still far from predominating even in ornamental beds. They were mainly grown in monastery gardens where medicinal, edible, and aromatic plants were cultivated, and where the few purely ornamental plants were of symbolic value.

From the tenth century onwards the Arab presence in southern Europe encouraged the development of botanical interests and the introduction of the first non-indigenous plant species. In the East, the garden had always been a place of spiritual life and was imbued with religious, poetic, and artistic symbolism. However, it was not until the sixteenth century that the first botanic gardens were laid out. They were linked to faculties of medicine, first at Padua and Pisa (1545), then in Montpellier (1593), Leyden, Oxford (1621) and at the Jardin du Roi in Paris (also 1621). At the same time, from the sixteenth century to the eighteenth century, the art of gardening was strongly influenced by both Italian Renaissance and formal French gardens. Architectural designs employed vegetation (trees, shrubs, clipped evergreens*) and stone, but left little room for flowers. Flowers were appreciated mainly by the collectors who grew and studied them.

Botanic gardens not only cultivated native plants but began adding species brought home by travellers, missionaries and merchants. Around 1590 the Jesuit Father André Thevet, chaplain to a company of Huguenots leaving for exile in Brazil, brought the first tobacco seeds back to France. Father d'Incarville, returning from a mission to Peking in 1687, introduced the peony, the incarvillea and the wisteria. A man called Flacourt, French commandant of the island of Madagascar, brought home a gardenia, a periwinkle and some immortelles in 1655. In 1703 Tournefort, botanist of the Jardin du Roi in France, brought back no less than one thousand three hundred and fifty-six plants from a long voyage in the Levant, including centaurea, valerian, acanthus and St John's wort. From the eighteenth century onwards there were more and more botanical expeditions. Exchanges with North America were extremely productive, and the collectors also returned with treasures from South America, Australia and South Africa. Peter Collinson, an English horticulturalist and collector, introduced an enormous number of North American species and exchanged plants with a New World

Brassicaceae
Cheiranthus cheiri 'Scarlet Emperor'
(Wallflower)
(x 1.5)

Asteraceae
Achillea 'Lachsschönheit'
(x 5)

nurseryman called Bartram. The French botanist Michaud spent over ten years collecting North American species for the Jardin des Plantes. Australian plants began arriving in Europe in the 1770s, after the expeditions of Joseph Banks and Captain Cook, but it was not until the nineteenth century that China and Japan finally opened up to the West, allowing the introduction of a considerable number of Asiatic plants.

A profusion of plants

The climate of England turned out to be particularly suitable for the establishment of these newcomers. Botanists amassed large collections and studied the behaviour of the newly introduced species. This was also the golden age of nurserymen, who themselves sent out expeditions all over the world and made a great many new plants available to amateur gardeners. The Loddiges of London were among the most famous of these nurserymen; they built up one of the biggest plant

collections in the world within a few decades. As early as 1823 the section of their catalogue covering herbaceous plants was offering fifty-two varieties of aconites, twenty-eight achilleas, eleven artemisias, forty-four Michaelmas daisies and twenty-five varieties of pinks. Gardening became an extremely popular hobby. More flowers were now being grown in gardens, while landscape gardeners and amateurs alike began making serious use of such perennials as stocks, campanulas, solidagos, aquilegias, Michaelmas daisies and evening primroses.

After the mid-nineteenth century, however, the great number of new glasshouses for raising plants, the wide choice of striking and brilliant plants now available – petunias, calceolarias, verbenas and other annuals – and their mass distribution by nurserymen led to a reduction in the range of plants grown. Landscape designers used flowers as bedding material, creating large expanses of rather glaring and monotonous colour. The romanticism of the eighteenth century was a thing of the past. This change has sometimes been described as the triumph of art and horticulture over nature.

In the 1870s the gardener and writer William Robinson mounted a vigorous attack on Victorian gardens of this kind. In her survey of his ideas, Penelope Hobhouse points out that he called for 'gardens composed of predominantly hardy plants – foreign plants were allowed as long as they behaved like natives and did not need special techniques of growing in the English climate ... The gardener had to understand where and how plants grew in the wild and then place them accordingly.'

Later another writer on horticulture, Shirley Hibberd, adopted Robinson's ideas and advised the introduction of a rustic atmosphere into the garden, making it attractive for the future as well as the present, and indeed throughout the year, with the emphasis on foliage plants. He recommended that gardeners plant a hardy herbaceous border. 'When well made, well stocked and well managed, it presents us with flowers in abundance during ten months out of twelve ... while the bedding system is an embellishment, the herbaceous border is a necessary fundamental feature.'

The career of Gertrude Jekyll is typical of this development in gardening theory. She saw the garden as a colour palette, and created a great many gardens in a free, natural, elegant style. Her writings are still a source of reference and inspiration for modern landscape designers. In a number of books and articles, she described the aesthetic and technical methods she used in adapting her style to very varied conditions of soil and climate, devising methods to allow a bolder choice of plants, and emphasising the aesthetic pleasure given by the combination of beautiful flowers and graceful foliage in borders of perennials composed in harmonious colours. As she said, writing in the *Journal of the Royal Horticultural Society* for 1891: 'An essential feature in a garden of hardy flowers is a well-arranged mixed border.'* Three decades later, she elaborated on these ideas: 'Where the better influences were at work to make us see the errors and deficiencies of the worst days of the bedding system, it was not a matter of destruction of the old ideals only, but a happy substitution of something saner and more satisfying; something of living hope and joy, a restitution of all that was best in the older gardening, with its scope ever widening as year by year more plants were introduced from all the world's temperate regions – from the Alps, the Cape, the Himalayas, the mountains of Western China, the uplands of South America, and other hitherto untapped sources.

Scrophulariaceae
Diascia 'Ruby Field'
(x 1.7)

Raisers of plants and seeds got to work to improve what was already known, and travellers engaged by enterprising firms to secure new species suitable for garden use.' (*Empire Review*, May 1924.)

As the advocates of a free, natural style of design, Robinson and his disciples, particularly Gertrude Jekyll, had a great influence on the history of English gardens. From the end of the nineteenth century onwards they were also influential in the United States and Europe. The general acceptance of perennials in the garden is largely due to them, and twentieth-century landscape designers have followed in their footsteps. In our own time, the wide availability of perennials and their increasing popularity with gardeners are still inspired by those English horticulturalists.

The same concept has brought an ecological dimension into the garden. In fact gardening is a good way of safeguarding nature, preserving species and re-creating a natural habitat. In the United States, landscape designers have laid out gardens to resemble nature reserves, in particular with the purpose of preserving the flora of the American prairies, and native plants play a major part. In modern Europe gardeners are increasingly anxious to use plants in the right way for their surroundings. The idea is to create a healthy environment, reduce reliance on mechanical and chemical methods of pest and disease control, and economise on water. Perennials have progressed far beyond the mixed border; garden designers today use them with great freedom and flexibility. The garden is becoming an ever-changing place allowing room for a certain natural wildness, and modern gardeners with forward-looking ideas tolerate a certain number of natural seedlings, accept colonising plants and will allow wild areas to become established. Most important of all, they take the time to look before they attempt to take control.

Amaryllidaceae
Alstroemeria aurantiaca
(x 0.9)

Fig. 1

Asteraceae

The older term Compositae is also in current use. This is the largest plant family of dicotyledons*, with about twenty-five thousand species throughout the world, most of them in temperate regions. Although the family includes so many species, all their flowers and inflorescences are constructed in such a similar way that there is no difficulty in recognising the relationship. What we initially perceive as the flower is actually a number of flowers uniting to form an inflorescence called a capitulum*. Most Asteaceae are herbaceous, and a good many are edible or medicinal; such plants include lettuce, artichoke, sunflower, arnica, camomile and pyrethrum. The family is full of treasures for the ornamental garden, providing a wealth of species which bear bright flowers over a long period, are easy to grow, and are very well adapted to European climates. Typical Asteraceae include ox-eye daisies, Michaelmas daisies, chrysanthemums, zinnias, marigolds, and dahlias.

FACING PAGE

Ratabida columnaris f. *pulcherrima*
(x 1.4)

The ratabida or Mexican hat has curious flower-heads with a pointed dark centre borne upright, while its long yellow or crimson petals droop down towards the ground. A plant in the rustic style, it makes a cheerful splash of colour in summer. It likes rather light, well-drained soil.

ORIGIN: North America
FLOWERING SEASON: June to September
HEIGHT: 0.7 m (26–28 in.)
SITUATION: sun
FROST-HARDY: ***
PROPAGATION: seed

Artemisia canescens
(x 2.5)

Artemisias are very interesting plants, particularly suited to dry soil. Their foliage is white, grey or silver, sometimes green, and they have divided, aromatic leaves which form very attractive and sculptural clumps or ground cover. This artemisia species has very finely divided leaves and a striking structural outline. A sub-shrubby, evergreen or sometimes semi-evergreen species, it prefers dry, well-drained soil.

FLOWERING SEASON: June to August
HEIGHT: 0.5 m (18–20 in.)
SITUATION: sun
FROST-HARDY: * * *
PROPAGATION: cuttings

Achillea filipendula
(x 0.9)

Achilleas are very rewarding plants. Easy to cultivate and free-flowering, they will grow in any kind of garden soil provided they are given a sunny position. Their umbelliferous* flower-heads are attractive in a flower-bed, as cut flowers, or in dried flower arrangements. With its large yellow inflorescences, *Achillea filipendulina* is an ideal plant for the back of a border.

ORIGIN: Caucasus
FLOWERING SEASON: June to July
HEIGHT: 1.2–1.5 m (4–5 ft)
SITUATION: sun
FROST-HARDY: * * *
PROPAGATION: division

Perennials

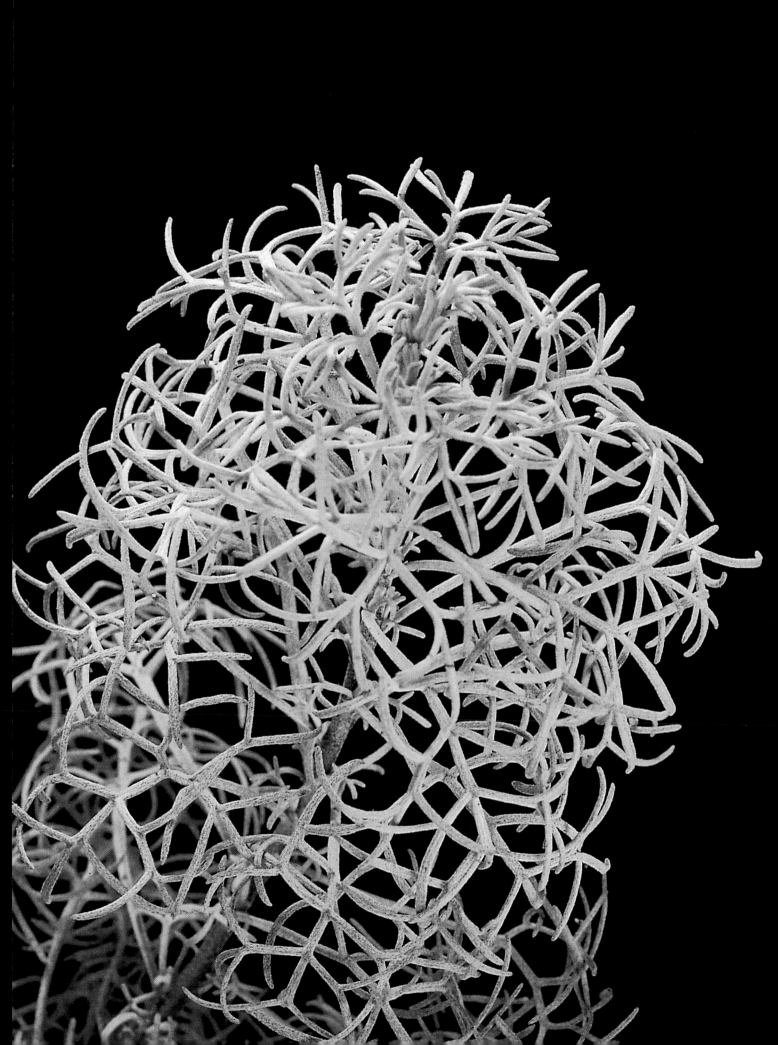

Catananche caerulea
(x 2.8)

A native of the Mediterranean area, the catananche loves sun and easily tolerates drought. It is a fine perennial, with foliage growing in a rosette shape and a beautiful blue inflorescence. It flowers at the end of spring, sometimes repeat-flowering in late summer. The flower-head is decorative when it fades, and since the silvery bracts do not drop but remain on the plant it can be used in dried flower arrangements. It will grow in rock gardens, on banks, or in well-drained flower-beds. Its life expectancy is medium.

FLOWERING SEASON: May to July
HEIGHT: 0.5 m (18–20 in.)
SITUATION: sun
FROST-HARDY: ***
PROPAGATION: seed

FACING PAGE

Aster novae-angliae 'Alma Pötschke'
(x 2.4)

A true cottage garden plant, the Michaelmas daisy is essential in autumn flower-beds. There are many cultivars. You can grow them in order of height, varying their colours. The Michaelmas daisy likes full sun and good garden soil that has not been allowed to dry out during summer.

FLOWER SEASON: September to October
HEIGHT: 1 m (38–40 in.)
SITUATION: sun
FROST-HARDY: ***
PROPAGATION: division

Chrysanthemum rubellum
'Clara Curtis'
(x 1.3)

A summer-flowering perennial with a delicate pink inflorescence and a yellow centre. It is effective in a sunny flower-bed of various shades of pink, or together with *Coreopsis verticillata* or *Ceratostigma plumbaginoides*.

FLOWERING SEASON: July to September
HEIGHT: 0.6 m (22–24 in.)
SITUATION: sun
FROST-HARDY: * * *
PROPAGATION: division

FACING PAGE

Echinacea angustifolia
(x 2.1)

This species has particularly fine, long, mauve ligulate florets with a more deeply coloured centre.

ORIGIN: Texas
FLOWERING SEASON: July to August
HEIGHT: 0.8 m (30–32 in.)
SITUATION: sun or partial shade
FROST-HARDY: * * *
PROPAGATION: division or seed

Echinacea purpurea
(x 2.5; x 1.5; x 3.2; x 1; x 0.5; x 0.9)

Echinacea, closely related to rudbeckia, is a very interesting genus and flowers freely in summer. The plant has strong stems, brightly coloured flowers shaped like the rays of the sun, and a curious protuberant centre. To be grown in deep, humus-rich soil.

ORIGIN: eastern North America
FLOWERING SEASON: July to September
HEIGHT: 0.8 m (30–32 in.)
SITUATION: sun or partial shade
FROST-HARDY: ***
PROPAGATION: division or seed

Gaillardia 'Burgunder'
(x 1.5)

The gaillardia is a hardy perennial, easy to grow and with a long flowering period in summer. It needs little water and prefers light soil and a sunny situation. The variety 'Burgunder' owes its name to its beautiful burnished colour, the red of Burgundy wine.

FLOWERING SEASON: June to August
HEIGHT: 0.6 m (22–24 in.)
SITUATION: sun
FROST-HARDY: * * *
PROPAGATION: seed

Helenium 'Moerheim Beauty'
(x 2.5)

A good perennial for flower-beds. It has a long flowering period in summer, with vibrantly coloured blooms, and is very hardy. 'Moerheim Beauty' is a hybrid in a warm shade of reddish orange. If planted in ordinary garden soil, it will need watering during the summer.

FLOWERING SEASON: June to August
HEIGHT: 0.9 m (34–36 in.)
SITUATON: sun
FROST-HARDY: * * *
PROPAGATION: division

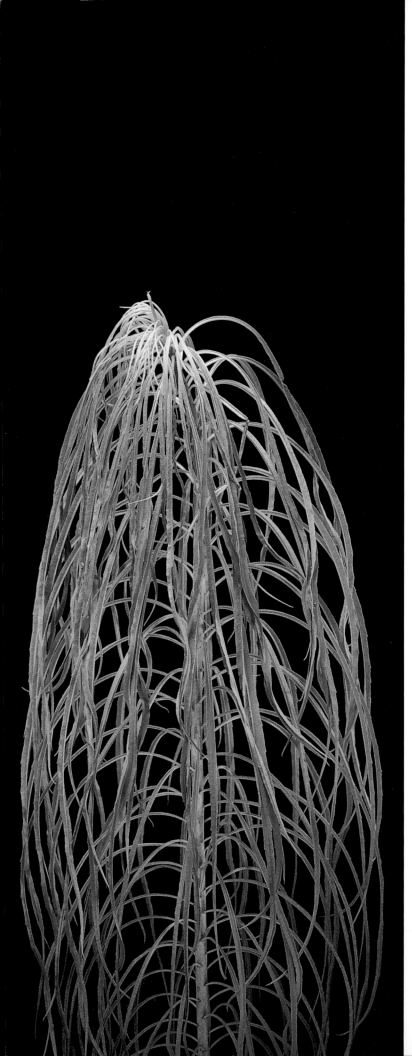

Helianthus salicifolius
(x 0.5)

This rhizomatous plant makes suckers*
producing new shoots and forms tall,
vigorous clumps. It is remarkable for its
long, fine, drooping foliage which moves
in the wind. The flowers are yellow,
loosely borne daisy heads. It tolerates
drought well, but will look more attractive
if it is kept well-watered in summer. It
needs plenty of space.

ORIGIN: North America
FLOWERING SEASON: August to September
HEIGHT: 2–2.5 m (6–8 ft)
SITUATION: sun
FROST-HARDY: ***
PROPAGATION: division

Helichrysum italicum
(x 1.9)

Syn.: *Helichrysum angustifolium*. Also known as the 'curry plant'. A shrubby, silver-leaved plant that retains its fine, dense foliage throughout the year and is highly aromatic. It grows well with other Mediterranean shrubs such as lavender, myrtle, dorycnium and ballota. It prefers well-drained or even dry soil and a position in full sun.

ORIGIN: Southern Europe
FLOWER SEASON: June to July
HEIGHT: 0.6 m (22–24 in.)
SITUATION: sun
FROST-HARDY: **
PROPAGATION: from cuttings

Liatris spicata
(x 1.2)

The liatris, also known as Blazing star, is a perennial with a tuberous rootstock, fine, linear, grass-like leaves, and thick stems surmounted by long, dense spikes of purplish pink flowers. Each spike flowers over a long period, beginning at the top. A plant to grow in the border or for cut flowers. It needs good garden soil and should be watered in summer.

ORIGIN: North America
FLOWER SEASONS: July to September
HEIGHT: 0.6 m (22–24 in.)
SITUATION: sun
FROST-HARDY: ***
PROPAGATION: division or seed

Stokesia laevis (x 2.4)

A plant with a spreading growth habit,
bright green lanceolate foliage and
large, deep blue capitulate flowers in
summer, with spiny bracts. It likes light
soil and is intolerant of lime.

ORIGIN: North America
FLOWERING SEASON: July to August
HEIGHT: 0.3 m (10–12 in.)
SITUATION: sun
FROST-HARDY: ***
PROPAGATION: division or seed

Tanacetum densum ssp. *amanii*
(x 1)

Syn.: *Chrysanthemum haradjanii.* Remark-able for its very pretty silver foliage, which is pinnate (finely divided like a bird's feather), this is a spreading ground-cover plant to be grown in a rockery or on well-drained soil. It tolerates drought well.

ORIGIN: Anatolia
FLOWERING SEASON: June to July
HEIGHT: 0.25 m (8–10 in.)
SITUATION: sun
FROST-HARDY: ***
PROPAGATION: division or cuttings

Asteraceae

Fig. 2

Lamiaceae

The term Labiatae is still often used for this plant family, which comprises about three thousand species of herbaceous perennials and sub-shrubs. They occur all over the world, but are mainly concentrated in Mediterranean areas. This is a very homogeneous family, and its members are easily identified: stems that are square in cross-section, with leaves arranged alternately, are a particularly characteristic feature. In most cases the asymmetrical flowers are arranged in glomerules (tufts) or false verticils (whorls) in the axils of the upper leaves. The glandulous hairs on all parts of the plants give them an aromatic scent. As a result, many Lamiaceae, including lavender, mint, basil, thyme, and patchouli, are grown for their scent and flavour. In a garden of perennials, species such as lamium, bugle and glechoma will provide ground cover, and species that will grow in dry conditions, including phlomis, sage and rosemary, are also useful.

FACING PAGE

Stachys byzantina
(x 3)

Syn.: *Stachys lanata*, also known as 'lambs' ears', and a very common garden plant. It has ground-cover foliage with erect flower spikes. It tolerates drought and can be grown on banks as a soil-retaining plant.

ORIGIN: the Mediterranean basin,
Asia Minor
FLOWERING SEASON: June to July
HEIGHT: 0.5 m (18–20 in.)
SITUATION: sun or partial shade
FROST-HARDY: ***
PROPAGATION: division or seed

Nepeta mussinii
(x 2.6)

Nepetas (catmint) are very useful perennials: they are vigorous, flower over a long period, and have aromatic foliage. This species harmoniously combines grey leaves with lavender-blue flowers, and if it is cut back after the first flush of flowering it will repeat-flower. With its cushion-forming growth habit, it makes an excellent edging plant and is a good plant for banks. Its flowering period is extended if it is kept well-watered in summer, and it will seed itself.

ORIGIN: Caucasus
FLOWERING SEASON: May to July, repeat-flowering
HAUTEUR: 0.3 m (10–12 in.)
EXPOSITION: sun
FROST-HARDY: ***
MULTIPLICATION: seed

BELOW

Marrubium cylleneum
(x 1)

A sub-shrubby plant with very attractive evergreen foliage. The leaves are rounded, downy and rimmed with silver. The plant has a spreading habit, and can be planted as ground cover on well-drained soil. It is ideal in a Mediterranean type of garden or a rockery.

ORIGIN: Mediterranean basin
FLOWERING SEASON: June to July
HEIGHT: 0.3 m (10–12 in.)
SITUATION: sun
FROST-HARDY: **
PROPAGATION: cuttings

Origanum tournefortii
(x 2)

Phlomis russeliana
(x 1.5)

A herbaceous perennial with evergreen foliage and a spreading root system. It forms a thick mat of large, broad, green leaves, more or less triangular in shape, and has a majestic presence. It will seed itself in the garden.

ORIGIN: Turkey
FLOWER SEASON: May to June
HEIGHT: 1m (38–40 in.)
SITUATION: sun
FROST-HARDY: ***
PROPAGATION: division

Syn.: *Origanum calcaratum.* Not to be confused with the European herb origanum, this species forms dense, low-growing tufts with many stems and small glaucous leaves. Its inflorescence is highly unusual, consisting as it does of interlocking pink-tinged bracts with small pink flowers emerging between them, giving the general effect of a lantern. Easy to grow in dry, well-drained soil in full sun, in the rockery, or as an edging plant for flower-beds. There are new hybrids in brighter colours.

ORIGIN: Crete, islands of the Aegean
FLOWERING SEASON: July to October
HEIGHT: 0.3 m (10–12 in.)
EXPOSITION: sun
FROST-HARDY: **
PROPAGATION: division or cuttings

Lamiaceae

Phlomis tuberosa
(x 0.5)

Both shrubby and herbaceous species of phlomis exist. They are well adapted to a Mediterranean climate. This species loses its wide crenate leaves in winter and has a robust tuberous rootstock.

ORIGIN: Southern Europe, Asia
FLOWERING SEASON: June to July
HEIGHT: 1 m (38–40 in.)
SITUATION: sun
FROST-HARDY: **
PROPAGATION: division or seed

Salvia argentea
(x 0.8)

Sages flower over a long period and are often very striking. Their foliage, whether deciduous* or evergreen, is usually highly aromatic. The leaves of this species are silvery and downy, forming a spreading rosette. It likes well-drained or dry soils and is short-lived, but can seed itself.

ORIGIN: Mediterranean
FLOWERING SEASON: May to June
HEIGHT: 0.7 m (26–28 in.)
SITUATION: sun
FROST-HARDY: **
PROPAGATION: seed

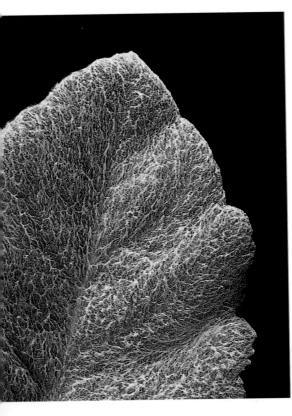

Salvia sclarea
(x 2.8)

Clary sage is a short-lived perennial and is often grown as a biennial, but it seeds itself easily. It is a fine plant with large, glaucous green leaves and large pink inflorescences with violet-blue bracts. Easy to grow, it forms handsome flowering clumps both in beds and borders.

ORIGIN: South-East Europe, South-West Asia
FLOWERING SEASON: June to July
HEIGHT: 1 m (38–40 in.)
SITUATION: sun
FROST-HARDY: ***
PROPAGATION: seed

Perennials

Salvia rutilans
(x 1.2)

The leaves of this species have a delicious pineapple scent, and its bright red inflorescence comes quite late in the year, bringing a welcome note of colour to the autumn garden. Unfortunately though, the flowers can be cut down by the first frosts. The plant dies back entirely in winter, and it is advisable to cover the rootstock with dry straw or bracken unless your garden is in a mild climate.

ORIGIN: Mexico
FLOWERING SEASON: September to October
HEIGHT: 0.6 m (22–24 in.)
SITUATION: sun or partial shade
FROST-HARDY: *
PROPAGATION: division or cuttings

FACING PAGE

Salvia uliginosa
(x 2.2)

A suckering herbaceous perennial. It produces many supple stems bearing long spikes of beautiful azure blue flowers throughout the summer. To make sure of a good show of flowers, plant this sage in deep soil and water it in very hot weather.

ORIGIN: Brazil
FLOWERING SEASON: June to August
HEIGHT: 1.5 m (5 ft)
SITUATION: sun
FROST-HARDY: *
PROPAGATION: division

Liliaceae

Most of the Liliaceae family are herbaceous perennials which survive the winter in European climates by means of their rhizomes, tubers or bulbs. They include lilies, lily of the valley and Solomon's seal. Only a few of the three thousand five hundred species in this family are woody and come from hotter regions; this minority of Liliaceae includes yucca, aloe and dracaena. The leaves of Liliaceae are usually long, narrow and with parallel veining. The foliage feeds the storage organs (rhizomes, bulbs) and in the case of herbaceous perennials dies back once it has fulfilled this function. Many species, such as tulips and lilies, have flowers with rich colouring. Others are grown for a variety of purposes: New Zealand flax (*Phormium tenax*) for its fibres; onions, garlic, leeks and asparagus for food, of course; aloes and colchicum for pharmaceutical use.

FACING PAGE

Hemerocallis 'Charlemagne'
(x 1.3)

FLOWERING SEASON: June to August
HEIGHT: 0.7 m (26–28 in.)
SITUATION: sun
FROST-HARDY: ***
PROPAGATION: division

Fig. 3

Hemerocallis 'Crimson Pirate'
(x 1.4)

Hemerocallis or day lilies are excellent
hardy perennials. They grow vigorously
and will be satisfied with ordinary garden
soil and moderate watering. Their
flowers do in fact resemble lilies, and
during summer they bear a profuse
succession of blooms. The huge number
of hybrids provides a wide colour range.
Day lilies can be grown together in beds
and borders, or used to good effect in
drifts at the edge of the garden.

FLOWERING SEASON: June to August
HEIGHT: 0.6 m (22–24 in.)
SITUATION: sun
FROST-HARDY: ***
PROPAGATION: division

Perennials

Hosta fortunei 'Albomarginata'
(x 1)

Hostas are elegant foliage plants of attractive shape, forming superb, vigorous clumps. There are many hosta varieties in different tones of blue and green or with variegated leaves, and interesting effects can be achieved by growing a number of them together. Although their fleshy roots enable them to tolerate drought, hostas will do best in humus-rich soil and a cool, moist position. A word of warning: slugs and snails adore them.

ORIGIN: China and Japan
FLOWERING SEASON: July to August
HEIGHT: 0.4–0.8 m (14–32 in.)
SITUATION: partial to full shade
FROST-HARDY: ***
PROPAGATION: division

Polygonatum odoratum
(x 0.7)

Solomon's seal is a delightful perennial for shady places or underplanting. Its arching stems bear finely veined leaves and white, bell-shaped flowers in spring. It is not particular about the kind of soil it likes, and it grows from fleshy rhizomes which give it good resistance to drought. Solomon's seal is attractive when grown with such ground-cover plants as pachysandra, lamium and violets.

ORIGIN: Europe
FLOWERING SEASON: April to May
HEIGHT: 0.5 m (18–20 in.)
SITUATION: partial shade
FROST-HARDY: ***
PROPAGATION: division

Kniphofia hybrids
(x 0.9)

Syn.: *Tritoma*. Also known as red-hot pokers, kniphofias are plants which form vigorous clumps, with lanceolate leaves and strong stems bearing conical orange inflorescences. If they are cut back after flowering they will repeat-flower. An interesting plant to grow at the back of the border, the kniphofia tolerates drought reasonably well.

ORIGIN: South Africa
FLOWERING SEASON: June to July
HEIGHT: 1–2 m (3–6 ft)
SITUATION: sun
FROST-HARDY: ***
PROPAGATION: division

Ophiopogon japonicus
(x 5.2)

The white flowers of this ophiopogon are followed by beautiful spherical, bright blue fruits. It is a rhizomatous plant forming tufts of deeply coloured, narrow evergreen leaves. Although it tolerates drought, it prefers a cool, moist position, where it will form attractive ground cover. It is often grown under trees and shrubs for that purpose.

ORIGIN: China and Japan
FLOWERING SEASON: June to July
HEIGHT: 0.3 m (10–12 in.)
SITUATION: partial shade
FROST-HARDY: **
PROPAGATION: division

Malvaceae

This family of plants mainly from the tropics contains about one thousand five hundred species of herbaceous perennials, shrubs and trees. Hibiscus and cotton are Malvaceae. Only a few species, such as mallows, grow in temperate and cool climates. The flowers of Malvaceae typically have five petals in an inflorescence where each petal both overlaps and is overlapped by another, and their numerous stamens are fused into a tube around the style (the hibiscus style is very characteristic). Malvaceae are good plants to grow in the ornamental garden. They have a long flowering period and are hardy, with an attractive simplicity of appearance and good resistance to drought. They include such flowers as lavatera, marsh mallow, hollyhock and malvastrum.

FACING PAGE

Malva sylvestris ssp. *mauritiana*
(x 1.3)

This vigorous mallow is an upright plant with large leaves. It is grown for the beautiful colour of its flowers. Although it tolerates drought, it will do best when grown in deep soil and watered in summer.

ORIGIN: Mediterranean
FLOWERING SEASON: June to September
HEIGHT: 1.2 m (4 ft)
SITUATION: sun or partial shade
FROST-HARDY: ***
PROPAGATION: seed

Abutilon megapotanicum
(x 1.3)

With its long, supple stems this plant can be fan-trained against a wall, allowed to trail over the ground, or staked to form a bush. It bears red and yellow bell-shaped flowers from June to the first frosts. It is evergreen in mild climates, and tolerates drought well.

ORIGIN: Brazil
FLOWERING SEASON: June to November
HEIGHT: depends on how it is grown
SITUATION: sun or partial shade
FROST-HARDY: *
PROPAGATION: cuttings

Lavatera thuringiaca
(x 2.2)

Lavatera is a popular genus because of its rapid growth, abundant flowers, good tolerance of drought, and the modest demands it makes on the soil. Unlike the shrubbier species of lavatera, this one has stems that die back every winter, leaving only a rosette of leaves. However, it grows very fast and flowers profusely in summer. Part of its charm is its tendency to seed itself even on the bleakest of slopes, where in fact it is often seen to its best advantage.

ORIGIN: Europe, Asia
FLOWERING SEASON: June to August
HEIGHT: 1.5 m (5 ft)
SITUATION: sun
FROST-HARDY: ***
PROPAGATION: cuttings or seed

Fig. 5

Papaveraceae

This family of about seven hundred species also includes the sub-family Fumariaceae, consisting of more elaborately developed Papaveraceae such as fumitory, corydalis and dicentra. The poppy sub-family consists of over four hundred species distributed throughout the temperate zones of the northern hemisphere. When the land bridges between the European and North American continents disappeared, the genera of Papaveraceae developed in different ways, producing Californian, Himalayan, and Oriental poppies. This family is of particular pharmaceutical importance because of the alkaloids contained in the latex of the plants. Their inflorescences are both simple and spectacular, and their handsome fruits, which develop as capsules or pods, make them very attractive garden plants even after flowering.

FACING PAGE

Glaucium corniculatum
(x 2)

The horned poppy is remarkable for the shape and bluish colour of its downy, crinkled leaves, and for its prickly flower buds and long seed-pods. Very tolerant of drought, it likes poor, well-drained soil. It can be a short-lived perennial, but it seeds itself readily in the garden.

ORIGIN: Southern Europe
FLOWERING SEASON: June to September
HEIGHT: 0.5 m (18–20 in.)
SITUATION: sun
FROST-HARDY: **
PROPAGATION: seed

Dicentra spectabilis
(x 4.2)

Everyone is familiar with 'bleeding heart', bearing its pretty bright pink, heart-shaped bells on graceful arched stems. The plant has fleshy roots which grow vigorously in humus-rich, light, cool, and moist soils. Its pretty bluish-green divided foliage often dies back in summer when the flowering period is over.

ORIGIN: China
FLOWERING SEASON: April to June
HEIGHT: 0.6 m (22–24 in.)
SITUATION: sun or partial shade
FROST-HARDY: ***
PROPAGATION: division

Romneya coulteri
(x 1.4)

The Californian poppy is a magnificent plant with glaucous foliage and large, white, scented flowers with yellow centres. It makes suckers, and is very drought-tolerant. Curiously, although this species can be invasive if it likes a garden, it can be difficult to establish, and first attempts to plant it do not always succeed. It needs sandy, well-drained soil, and does not respond well to transplanting.

ORIGIN: California
FLOWERING SEASON: June to September
HEIGHT: 1.5 m (5 ft)
SITUATION: sun
FROST-HARDY: **
PROPAGATION: division or seed

ABOVE

Macleaya cordata
(x 0.7)

Syn.: *Bocconia cordata*. A very vigorous rhizomatous plant that produces an abundance of tall, architectural stems every spring. It is also notable for its divided foliage and misty russet-coloured flower-heads. It does best in deep soil and is ideal in a foliage garden or at the back of a border.

ORIGIN: China
FLOWERING SEASON: July to August
HEIGHT: 2 m (6 ft)
SITUATION: sun or partial shade
FROST-HARDY: ***
PROPAGATION: division

Perennials

Oenotheraceae

This family comprises six hundred and fifty species, most of them natives of the temperate and sub-tropical regions of the American continent. They are either herbaceous (epilobium and oenothera species) or shrubs (fuchsia). The herbaceous species have proved particularly good at colonising other temperate regions. When their long, slender fruits are ripe they shed many seeds which are easily dispersed. Evening primrose (*Oenothera biennis*) has become naturalised in Europe in this way, while *Jussiaea repens* has invaded the streams and rivers of the south of France. The Oenotheraceae plant family has adapted well to the climatic conditions of European gardens. Its members are easily grown and look attractive in a cottage garden. They have a long flowering period in summer, and increase easily by seeding themselves or making suckers (in the case of species such as gaura, oenothera and zauschneria).

FACING PAGE

Fuchsia magellanica 'Riccartonii'
(x 2.5)

This very hardy fuchsia can be planted in the open ground. In a mild climate it will make a bush; in a colder climate it will die back and grow again from the rootstock every spring. Its long flowering season makes it a popular plant for summer. It grows best in well-drained soil.

ORIGIN: South America
FLOWERING SEASON: June to October
HEIGHT: 1 m (38–40 in.)
SITUATION: sun or partial shade
FROST-HARDY: **
PROPAGATION: cuttings

Zauschneria californica
(x 4)

A suckering plant that throws up stems from a woody rootstock. The stems themselves are semi-woody, bearing small, bright green, deciduous leaves. It is interesting for its charming bright orange-red flowers, borne throughout the summer. *Zauschneria* likes a hot position and well-drained, stony soil. It dislikes cold, wet winters, and in such weather it is advisable to cover the rootstock with straw. Prune back the dry stems at the end of winter.

ORIGIN: California
FLOWERING SEASON: July to October
HEIGHT: 0.5 m (18–20 in.)
SITUATION: sun
FROST-HARDY: **
PROPAGATION: division or cuttings

ABOVE

Gaura lindheimeri
(x 1)

The long, supple stems of this beautiful plant bear delicate white flowers with a pink calyx throughout the summer. It is an easy perennial, and will grow vigorously in well-drained soil. It seeds itself lavishly.

ORIGIN: southern United States
FLOWERING SEASON: June to October
HEIGHT: 1 m (38–40 in.)
SITUATION: sun
FROST-HARDY: ***
PROPAGATION: seed

RIGHT

Oenothera speciosa
(x 0.9)

Oenotheras have adapted well to European climates and are drought-tolerant. They bear a wealth of flowers in various colours. This creeping species makes suckers producing many upright stems, and can rapidly colonise banks and flower-beds. It has enchanting flowers of a delicate, pale pink.

ORIGIN: North America
FLOWERING SEASON: June to September
HEIGHT: 0.4 m (14–16 in.)
SITUATION: sun
FROST-HARDY: **
PROPAGATION: division or cuttings

Ranunculaceae

This is a large family of one thousand eight hundred species, the majority of them native to the temperate and cool regions of the northern hemisphere. It is well represented among the wild flowers of Europe by such plants as buttercups, anemones, celandines and hellebores. A sequence of evolution can be traced in the family, which contains some species of primitive structure and others that are more highly developed, with many intermediate species in between. As a result there are few characteristics in common to all its genera. Many members of this family are herbaceous perennials, often with a rhizomatous rootstock. They have been grown in ornamental gardens for a very long time, and are represented by such widely differing genera as peonies, delphiniums, hellebores, anemones, aquilegias, and aconites.

FACING PAGE

Aquilegia chrysantha
(x 2.5)

Aquilegias like cool, moist soil and a sunny position, but will also grow in partial shade. Besides the botanical species, there are many brightly coloured, spurred and ruffled cultivated varieties. The divided green leaves, sometimes tinged with blue, are also extremely decorative.

ORIGIN: southern United States
FLOWERING SEASON: May to July
HEIGHT: 0.8 m (30–32 in.)
SITUATION: sun or partial shade
FROST-HARDY: ***
PROPAGATION: seed

Anemone hupehensis 'Splendens'
(x 1.8)

The autumn anemone is perfect for colonising a shady part of the garden, where it will flourish. Its delicate pink or white flowers perched on slender, supple stems are a most attractive sight. It does not need a great deal of water, and it easily increases itself. The general term 'Japanese anemone' covers *Anemone hupehensis*, *Anemone* x *hybrida* and their varieties.

ORIGIN: China
FLOWERING SEASON: August to October
HEIGHT: 0.8 m (30–32 in.)
SITUATION: partial to full shade
FROST-HARDY: ***
PROPAGATION: division

Aquilegia vulgaris 'Nora Barlow'
(x 2.4)

This aquilegia has a shaggy double
flower with petals of an old rose shade.

FLOWERING SEASON: April to May
HEIGHT: 0.8 m (30–32 in.)
SITUATION: sun or partial shade
FROST-HARDY: ***
PROPAGATION: seed

FACING PAGE

Aquilegia flabellata
(x 2.8)

With its blue and white flowers, this
short-growing aquilegia is a delightful
plant for a rockery.

ORIGIN: Japan
FLOWERING SEASON: April to May
HEIGHT: 0.3 m (10–12 in.)
SITUATION: sun or partial shade
FROST-HARDY: ***
PROPAGATION: seed

Delphinium Pacific Hybrids
(x 3.4)

The perennial larkspur is a fine plant for
the back of a border, with its height and
its magnificent flower spikes in various
shades of blue, pink, purple, or white. It
needs deep soil and a position sheltered
from the wind.

FLOWERING SEASON: June to July, sometimes
repeat-flowering in
September
HEIGHT: 1.5–2 m (5–6 ft)
SITUATION: sun
FROST-HARDY: ***
PROPAGATION: seed

Helleborus argutifolius
(x 0.6)

Syn.: *Helleborus corsicus*. This species is quite tall and still has something of the look of a wild flower. It has pale green trilobate leaves, leathery and spiny, and cup-shaped yellowish green flowers. Easy to grow in well-drained soil, its graceful shape adds an attractive touch to the winter garden.

ORIGIN: Corsica
FLOWERING SEASON: January to April
HEIGHT: 0.6 m (22–24 in.)
SITUATION: partial shade
FROST-HARDY: **
PROPAGATION: seed

Paeonia lactiflora 'Sarah Bernhardt'
(x 1)

Peonies are very popular with most gardeners. Besides the botanical species, there is a wide range of different hybrids. Peonies like deep, humus-rich soil that does not dry out too much in summer. Their fleshy rootstocks should be planted just below the soil surface, and transplanting them is inadvisable; the peony does not like being disturbed. 'Sarah Bernhardt' is quite an old hybrid, bred by Lemoine in 1906.

ORIGIN: East Asia
FLOWERING SEASON: June
HEIGHT: 0.9 m (34–36 in.)
SITUATION: sun or partial shade
FROST-HARDY: ***
PROPAGATION: division

Trollius chinensis 'Golden Queen'
(x 2.8)

The trollius or globeflower likes rich, cool, moist soil. Its pretty cup-shaped orange-yellow flowers are similar to those of buttercups.

ORIGIN: China
FLOWERING SEASON: July to August
HEIGHT: 0.6 m (22–24 in.)
SITUATION: sun or partial shade
FROST-HARDY: ***
PROPAGATION: division

LEFT

Pulsatilla vulgaris 'Rubra'
(x 2.2)

It is a joy to see the pretty purple, red, or white flowers of the pulsatilla or Pasque flower, a type of anemone, appearing at the end of winter. The stamens are golden yellow and the leaves finely divided. Pulsatillas tolerate drought well and are excellent for a rockery.

ORIGIN: Europe
FLOWERING SEASON: February to March
HEIGHT: 0.3 m (10–12 in)
SITUATION: sun or partial shade
FROST-HARDY: ***
PROPAGATION: seed

Perennials

Fig. 8

Saxifragaceae

This family contains over a thousand species, mostly distributed in temperate climates of the northern hemisphere – some are natives to mountainous areas – and extending into Arctic zones. A distinction should be drawn between shrubs (syringa, hydrangea, deutzia, currant) and herbaceous perennials. The genus *Saxifraga* alone contains over three hundred species. Lovers of perennials will also be well acquainted with bergenias, heucheras, tiarellas, rodgersias and other members of this family that do well in cool gardens.

FACING PAGE

Saxifraga x *urbium* 'Aureopunctata'
(x 2.9)

The saxifrage genus contains species of various origins, most of them natives of the mountains. So long as they have a certain amount of humidity or a cool atmosphere, they can be established in shallow soils, on rockeries, and among rocks. This species has fleshy leaves of medium size blotched with yellow, growing in rosettes to make dense mats.

FLOWERING SEASON: May to June
HEIGHT: 0.6 m (22–24 in.)
SITUATION: partial shade
FROST-HARDY: ***
PROPAGATION: division or cuttings

Astilbe japonica 'Deutschland'
(x 0.8)

The inflorescences of astilbes are very characteristic. They consist of panicles borne at the top of the flower stem, either drooping or erect, in luminous, almost glowing colours. There are many white, pink or red hybrids. The leaves, divided to a greater or lesser extent, are dense and shiny. These are plants for a rich, cool, moist soil, and ideal for marginal planting round a pond.

FLOWERING SEASON: June to July
HEIGHT: 0.5 m (18–20 in.)
SITUATION: partial to full shade
FROST-HARDY: ***
PROPAGATION: division

RIGHT

Bergenia cordifolia
(x 1.7)

The bergenia is a typical easily grown perennial, at home in every garden. Its large round, leathery, shiny leaves form thick evergreen mats that take on a reddish tinge in winter. The pretty pink flowers appear in early spring. A very hardy plant, the bergenia will grow anywhere, and can be used as an edging plant, in a cold, shady corner, or for planting in large containers.

ORIGIN: Siberia
FLOWERING SEASON: February to April
HEIGHT: 0.3–0.5 m (10–20 in.)
SITUATION: sun or partial to full shade
FROST-HARDY: ***
PROPAGATION: division

Heuchera 'Bressingham'
(x 1.1)

This plant has delicate little flowers of a subtle red colour, borne erect. Its evergreen heart-shaped leaves form a thick carpet and may be blotched with red. Although it tolerates drought it will grow better in cool, moist soil.

FLOWERING SEASON: May to July
HEIGHT: 0.5 m (18–20 in.)
SITUATION: sun or partial shade
FROST-HARDY: ***
PROPAGATION: division or seed

Saxifraga x *arendsii* (x 3.6)

This species has finely divided leaves forming dense, light green cushions. Its flowers are a particularly intense shade of ruby red.

FLOWERING SEASON: May to June
HEIGHT: 0.15 m (5–6 in.)
SITUATION: partial shade
FROST-HARDY: ***
PROPAGATION: division or cuttings

Saxifragaceae

Solanaceae

The Solanaceae family contains about two thousand five hundred species, natives of warm and temperate regions, the majority coming from Central and South America. Potatoes, aubergines, tomatoes and sweet peppers are all Solanaceae. The genus *Solanum* alone contains about two thousand species, including the potato. The family also includes many medicinal plants, rich in alkaloids and often toxic, such as belladonna, henbane, thorn-apple and tobacco. Solanaceae are herbaceous perennials or semi-woody sub-shrubs, often making large, strong plants. A distinction is drawn between species with berries and regular flowers (such as those of the easily identifiable *Solanum* genus), species with seed capsules and regular flowers (tobacco, datura) and species with more or less irregular flowers (petunia). Many Solanaceae are grown as annuals in European climates. Only a few species will tolerate winter frosts.

FACING PAGE

Nicotiana sylvestris
(x 2.2)

Although flowering tobacco is often grown as an annual, it is a perennial species in most European regions. It has large, rough leaves and tubular white flowers with a delicious scent. It prefers fertile, deep, well-drained soil, where it will seed itself readily.

ORIGIN: Argentina
FLOWERING SEASON: July to September
HEIGHT: 0.9 m (34–36 in.)
SITUATION: sun or partial shade
FROST-HARDY: ***
PROPAGATION: seed

ABOVE

Jaborosa integrifolia
(x 0.9)

With its exquisite, unusual little flowers
consisting of five spurred pure white
petals, and its attractive broad leaves, this
rhizomatous creeping plant makes pretty
ground cover on ordinary but preferably
well-drained garden soil.

ORIGIN: South America
FLOWERING SEASON: June to September
HEIGHT: 0.25 m (8–10 in.)
SITUATION: sun or partial shade
FROST-HARDY: **
PROPAGATION: division

RIGHT

Datura meteloides
(x 1)

Daturas are fascinating plants with
beautiful flowers and an enchanting
scent. Unfortunately they contain a great
many alkaloids, and are toxic. They need
a mild climate. *Datura meteloides* is one of
the hardiest species. It can survive mild
winters in the open ground in a
sheltered situation or covered with straw.
It will also seed itself in the garden. This
species has bushy growth, greyish, downy
leaves, and many scented, trumpet-
shaped flowers borne erect.

ORIGIN: Texas and California
FLOWERING SEASON: July to September
HEIGHT: 1 m (38–40 in.)
SITUATION: warm and sunny
FROST-HARDY: *
PROPAGATION: seed

Perennials

Solanaceae

Solanum mauritianum
(x 0.8)

Syn.: *Solanum auriculatum.* This remarkable and rather exotic plant has broad, downy greyish leaves, strong branching stems covered with hairs, and a sprawling, bushy growth habit. It is vigorous, and produces suckers. The purple flowers, arranged in corymbs*, are followed by spherical orange fruits. It likes a warm position sheltered from the wind and winter frosts, in well-drained soil. It is advisable to cover it with straw in winter.

FLOWERING SEASON: July to October
HEIGHT: 2 m (6 ft)
SITUATION: full sun
FROST-HARDY: *
PROPAGATION: division or seed

Physalis franchetii
(x 3)

Also known as Japanese lantern, the physalis is an easy perennial to grow. It increases rapidly, thanks to its creeping, fleshy roots. The white flowers are insignificant, but the fruits that follow are contained in a striking, papery orange calyx. At this stage of development the stems can be cut to make beautiful dried flower arrangements. The plant can be invasive in rich soil.

ORIGIN: Japan
FLOWERING SEASONS: June to July
HEIGHT: 0.6 m (22–24 in.)
SITUATION: sun
FROST-HARDY: ***
PROPAGATION: division

Perennials

Fig. 10

Other genera and species

Flowering plants, or angiosperms*, trees, shrubs, and herbaceous plants, form a vast group of over two hundred thousand species and more than three hundred plant families – further evidence of the great diversity of vegetation growing on this planet. The perennials presented in this book embrace some forty families of various origins. While some plant families, for instance Asteraceae and Ranunculaceae, are very well represented in gardens, others are grown on a smaller scale in European climates or hardly at all, while sometimes only a very few genera or species can adapt to our gardens. Their rarity makes them even more remarkable, and they make a valuable contribution to the diversity of their surroundings.

FACING PAGE

Acanthaceae
Acanthus spinosus
(x 2.5)

In mild climates the acanthus is a useful plant for colonising difficult areas (dry and shady parts of the garden, north-facing areas that get little sun). It has beautiful bright green leaves forming ground cover, and striking flower spikes. When the seeds are ripe they will disperse themselves all over the garden.

ORIGIN: southern Italy, the Balkans
FLOWERING SEASON: June to July
HEIGHT: 1.5 m (5 ft)
SITUATION: sun or partial to full shade
FROST-HARDY: **
PROPAGATION: seed

Aizoaceae
Delosperma cooperi
(x 2.5)

Delospermas belong to the same family as purslane and other succulents. They have the exotic appearance of the plant family in general, but are notable for their good tolerance of cold. They make excellent ground cover on dry soil, colonising it by putting out runners*. *Delosperma cooperi* has small, long, fleshy leaves. Its flowers are carried in profusion. The plant likes well-drained soil and a warm, sunny position.

ORIGIN: South Africa
FLOWERING SEASON: June to September
HEIGHT: 0.05 m (2 in.)
SITUATION: sun
FROST-HARDY: **
PROPAGATION: cuttings

Acanthaceae
Jacobinia suberecta
(x 2)

Attractively combining velvety grey-green leaves and orange flowers, this perennial is worth growing for its long flowering season in summer and its good tolerance of drought. It likes a warm position with well-drained soil in winter. The jacobinia deserves to be more widely grown in mild climates, but needs protection in cold areas.

ORIGIN: Uruguay
FLOWERING SEASON: July to September
HEIGHT: 0.4 m (14–16 in.)
SITUATION: sun
FROST-HARDY: *
PROPAGATION: cuttings

Perennials

Apocynaceae
Vinca major 'Variegata'
(x 1.3)

Periwinkles are extremely useful ground-cover perennials. They increase from suckers, have evergreen foliage, and make dense carpets enlivened by their pretty flowers in spring. They tolerate drought well in summer. The variegated periwinkle is particularly vigorous and may even be invasive on rich soil.

FLOWERING SEASON: March to April
HEIGHT: 0.5 m (18–20 in.)
SITUATION: partial to full shade
FROST-HARDY: ***
PROPAGATION: division or cuttings

FACING PAGE

Campanulaceae
Campanula takesimana
(x 2.1)

Campanulas are a huge genus, familiar to all of us from the gardens and the countryside we knew in childhood. They are easy to grow. This beautiful species has white or pink flowers blotched with purple, borne at the end of flexible stems. It spreads by suckers and is best in cool, moist soil.

ORIGIN: Korea
FLOWERING SEASON: June to July
HEIGHT: 0.6 m (22–24 in.)
SITUATION: sun or partial shade
FROST-HARDY: ***
PROPAGATION: division

Perennials

Campanulaceae
Platycodon grandiflorus
(x 0.8)

The platycodon, a close relative of the campanulas, is notable for the purity of outline of its flowers and the curious shape of its flower buds. It has fleshy roots and needs deep, well-drained soil. It bears beautiful blue flowers in summer, and will repeat-flower if the faded blooms are dead-headed. There are white, pink, and purple varieties.

ORIGIN: China and Japan
FLOWERING SEASON: July to September
HEIGHT: 0.6 m (22–24 in.)
SITUATION: sun or partial shade
FROST-HARDY: ***
PROPAGATION: division or seed

FACING PAGE

Campanulaceae
Lobelia laxiflora (x 1.7)

A plant with a spreading, suckering, and vigorous habit of growth, this lobelia has fine, pale green leaves and red and yellow bell-shaped flowers. It tolerates drought well. It needs well-drained soil, and the rootstock should be protected in winter in cold areas.

ORIGIN: Mexico
FLOWERING SEASON: June to September
HEIGHT: 0.5 m (18–20 in.)
SITUATION: sun or partial shade
FROST-HARDY: *
PROPAGATION: division

RIGHT

Convolvulaceae
Convolvulus mauritanicus (x 1.2)

A remarkable ground-cover plant. It flowers profusely, and has small, round, semi-evergreen leaves which will cascade over a small wall or the sides of a container. It needs protection when grown in well-drained soil in cold areas.

ORIGIN: North Africa
FLOWERING SEASON: May to September
HEIGHT: 0.15 m (5–6 in.)
SITUATION: sun
FROST-HARDY: *
PROPAGATION: cuttings

Other genera and species

Commelinaceae
Tradescantia x *andersonia* 'Karminglut' (x 1.8)

The tradescantia, a pretty, deciduous perennial, spreads by suckers and has narrow leaves and charming three-petalled flowers. It is easy to grow but prefers cool, moist soil. 'Karminglut' is a carmine-pink hybrid. There are many other hybrids, ranging in colour from white to purple.

FLOWERING SEASON: May to July
HEIGHT: 0.3 m (10–12 in.)
SITUATION: sun or partial shade
FROST-HARDY: ***
PROPAGATION: by division

Cistaceae
Helianthemum 'Fire Dragon' (x 1.5)

Helianthemums like warm, dry positions, and will grow among rocks or dunes. There are many hybrids with bright flowers and leaves in delicate shades. They are spreading, shrubby ever-greens that form carpets or cascade over a low wall.

FLOWERING SEASON: April to June, with some repeat flowering
HEIGHT: 0.2 m (6–8 in.)
SITUATION: sun
FROST-HARDY: ***
PROPAGATION: cuttings

Perennials

Crassulaceae
Sedum kamtschaticum 'Variegatum'
(x 2.2)

Sedums are a huge genus, widely distributed all over the world, and generally found in light, well-drained or even dry soils. Their fleshy leaves sometimes persist throughout winter, and they always remain decorative. This low-growing species is a ground-cover plant suitable for a rockery.

FLOWERING SEASON: June to July
HEIGHT: 0.15 m (5–6 in.)
SITUATION: sun
FROST-HARDY: ***
PROPAGATION: cuttings

Dipsaceae
Morina longifolia
(x 1.1)

This plant, with its prickly leaves and curious flower spikes, is very aromatic. It needs soil that is well drained in winter but not too dry in summer.

ORIGIN: Himalayas
FLOWERING SEASON: June to July
HEIGHT: 0.3–0.5 m (10–20 in.)
SITUATION: sun
FROST-HARDY: **
PROPAGATION: seed

Euphorbiaceae
Euphorbia amygdaloides
var. *robbiae*
(x 1.7)

Euphorbias are a very decorative genus. Both their foliage and their curious flowerlike bracts are interesting in structure. They are natives of a number of different places, and while some have adapted to poor, dry soils others need a cool, moist position. This species has bright green leaves which are evergreen and very attractive. It is a suckering plant, useful for colonising a shady place, and will tolerate drought quite well.

ORIGIN: Turkey
FLOWERING SEASON: April to May
HEIGHT: 0.4 m (14–16 in.)
SITUATION: partial to full shade
FROST-HARDY: **
PROPAGATION: division

FACING PAGE

Euphorbiaceae
Euphorbia myrsinites
(x 2.2)

An excellent rockery plant of spreading habit and with unusual evergreen leaves, scaly and tinged with grey-blue. It tolerates drought well and will seed itself in the garden.

ORIGIN: Crimea, Balkans, Italy
FLOWERING SEASON: April to May
HEIGHT: 0.2 m (6–8 in.)
SITUATION: sun
FROST-HARDY: ***
PROPAGATION: from seed

Geraniaceae
Geranium macrorrhizum (x 2.9)

This vigorous rhizomatous ground-cover plant has ever-green foliage, with downy, aromatic leaves, above which magenta flowers open from red calyces.

ORIGIN: Balkans
FLOWERING SEASON: April to June
HEIGHT: 0.3 m (10–12 in.)
SITUATION: sun or partial shade
FROST-HARDY: ***
PROPAGATION: division

BELOW

Geraniaceae
Geranium 'Johnson's Blue' (x 1.1)

There are many species of perennial geraniums, easy to grow and bearing a wealth of flowers in various colours. Geraniums have many uses: in beds and borders, on rockeries or as ground-cover plants. This variety, popular for its large, deep blue flowers, forms attractive clumps. The leaves are deeply lobed and toothed.

FLOWERING SEASON: June to July
HEIGHT: 0.4 m (14–16 in.)
SITUATION: sun or partial shade
FROST-HARDY: ***
PROPAGATION: division

ABOVE

Fabaceae
Lupinus Russell Hybrids
(x 0.3)

Lupins are among the best-known of cottage garden plants, and are still very popular. It must be admitted that their flower spikes are spectacular and their leaves very decorative; in addition, there is a wide variety of hybrids in different colours. But they are not easy to grow, and need deep, light, preferably sandy soil. They do not tolerate lime.

FLOWERING SEASON: May to July
HEIGHT: 0.8 m (30–32 in.)
SITUATION: sun or partial shade
FROST-HARDY: ***
PROPAGATION: seed

Iridaceae
Crocosmia 'Lucifer' (x 1.1)

The crocosmia is related to the gladiolus, but has a much more delicate inflorescence, which is borne with particular elegance above slender, erect foliage. 'Lucifer' is a lovely bright red. This bulbous plant will increase easily in the garden, where it survives the winter without difficulty except in cold, wet areas.

FLOWERING SEASON: June to July
HEIGHT: 1 m (38–40 in.)
SITUATION: sun
FROST-HARDY: **
PROPAGATION: division

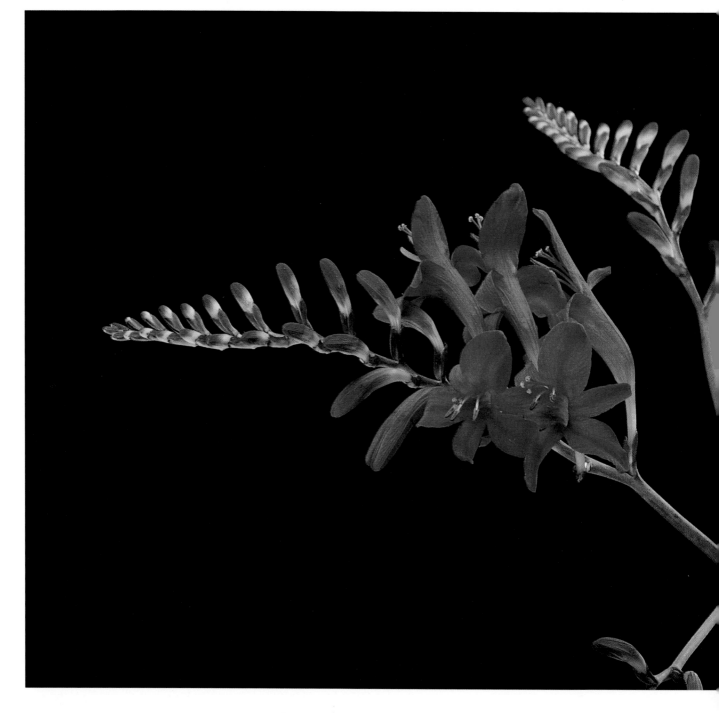

Iridaceae
Schizostylis coccinea 'Major' (x 1.1)

Also known as Kaffir lily, this is a bulbous plant with beautiful flowers resembling small lilies in autumn. It will increase easily in cool, moist garden soil.

FLOWERING SEASON: September to November
HEIGHT: 0.6 m (22–24 in.)
SITUATION: sun
FROST-HARDY: **
PROPAGATION: division

Other genera and species

Iridaceae
Sisyrinchium angustifolium
(x 3)

Syn.: *Sisyrinchium bermudianum.* These are interesting plants for a rockery, forming small clumps of fine, narrow leaves like the leaves of a miniature iris, from which the stems emerge and bear glowing flowers in late spring and early summer. This species is notable for its blue flowers with their yellow centres.

ORIGIN: eastern North America
FLOWERING SEASON: May to June
HEIGHT: 0.25 m (8–10 in.)
SITUATION: sun
FROST-HARDY: **
PROPAGATION: division or seed

Poaceae
Miscanthus saccharifolius
(x 0.4)

This vigorous grass is very ornamental in the garden. It makes tall clumps with fine, drooping leaves and inflorescences that fade but remain on the plant and, once they have dried out, are decorative all through the winter. It likes deep, rather cool, moist soils, and has attractive reddish autumn colouring.

ORIGIN: Asia
FLOWERING SEASON: August to September
HEIGHT: 2 m (6 ft)
SITUATION: sun or partial shade
FROST-HARDY: ***
PROPAGATION: division

Melianthaceae
Melianthus major
(x 0.4)

A magnificent plant, with striking toothed foliage which remains on the plant in mild winters, when it may grow to 2 m (6 ft). In colder situations (below about 7° C), it dies back and comes up again from the rootstock in spring. Reddish brown flowers are borne on stems that survive the winter. To be grown in ordinary garden soil.

ORIGIN: South Africa
FLOWERING SEASON: April to May
HEIGHT: 1.2 m (4 ft)
SITUATION: sun
FROST-HARDY: **
PROPAGATION: division

Other genera and species

Plumbaginaceae
Ceratostigma plumbaginoides
(x 3.9)

Syn.: *Plumbago larpentae*. A vigorous, deciduous, suckering ground-cover plant. It tolerates drought well, and is popular because of its long flowering season. It has a place in every garden, and is indispensable for colonising difficult areas, in particular the edges of paving or walls.

ORIGIN: Western China
FLOWERING SEASON: August to October
HEIGHT: 0.3 m (10–12 in.)
SITUATION: sun or partial shade
FROST-HARDY: ***
PROPAGATION: division or cuttings

Primulaceae
Dodecatheon meadia
(x 2.4)

Also known as shooting star, this plant is popular for its unusual little flowers with reflexed petals like those of the cyclamen. It grows slowly, and its foliage dies down in summer, so care must be taken to protect it from any competition from neighbouring plants until it is well established. It likes cool, moist soils.

ORIGIN: North America
FLOWERING SEASON: May to June
HEIGHT: 0.3 m (10–12 in.)
SITUATION: sun or partial shade
FROST-HARDY: ***
PROPAGATION: division

BELOW

Portulaceae
Calandrinia umbellata
(x 2.1)

A small plant with cushion-forming foliage from which pretty cup-shaped flowers rise. They are bright carmine pink, and are suitable for growing on a warm, well-drained rockery.

ORIGIN: Chile
FLOWERING SEASON: June to September
HEIGHT: 0.2 m (6–8 in.)
SITUATION: sun
FROST-HARDY: *
PROPAGATION: seed

Perennials

Rosaceae
Alchemilla mollis
(x 1.5)

Alchemilla or lady's mantle has beautiful pale green, almost downy foliage. Drops of water roll off the leaves like quicksilver. The inflorescence forms a sulphur-yellow head that lasts all summer. Alchemilla is an excellent ground-cover plant for beds and borders. It also makes a good plant for filling in any spaces left empty in a garden design, and can be useful to soften a rather rigid design or to set off other perennials. It likes cool, moist soil.

ORIGIN: South-east Europe
FLOWERING SEASON: June to August
HEIGHT: 0.4 m (14–16 in.)
SITUATION: sun or partial shade
FROST-HARDY: ***
PROPAGATION: division or seed

Saururaceae
Houttuynia cordata 'Chameleon'
(x 1.9)

This curious suckering ground-cover plant has multicoloured leaves in shades of red, green, yellow, and cream, and is useful for colonising cool, moist areas, or even for growing in shallow water.

ORIGIN: China and Japan
FLOWERING SEASON: May to June
HEIGHT: 0.3 m (10–12 in.)
SITUATION: partial to full shade
FROST-HARDY: ***
PROPAGATION: division

Other genera and species

Scrophulariaceae
Phygelius capensis
(x 1.6)

A semi-woody plant, also known as Cape fuchsia, with an interesting and rather exotic-looking structure. The coral-red tubular flowers are arranged in loose inflorescences at the tops of the stems. The phygelius likes light soil in a warm position, ideally against a wall.

ORIGIN: South Africa
FLOWERING SEASON: July to September
HEIGHT: 1.5 m (5 ft)
SITUATION: sun or partial shade
FROST-HARDY: **
PROPAGATION: division or cuttings

Scrophulariaceae
Penstemon 'Souvenir d'Adrien Régnier'
(x 1.6)

With their attractive flowers, vigour, and rapid growth, penstemon hybrids are excellent perennials. They form basket-shaped sub-shrubby plants crowned with tubular snapdragon flowers in bright colours. They will be happy with ordinary garden soil, and can tolerate drought. In winter they need well-drained soil and protection from frost.

FLOWERING SEASON: June to September
HEIGHT: 0.3–0.5 m (10–20 in.)
SITUATION: sun
FROST-HARDY: **
PROPAGATION: division or cuttings

Valerianaceae
Centranthus ruber
(x 0.4)

The valerian does very well in dry, sunny gardens. Its pale green leaves are slightly fleshy, and its flowers, which are very pure in colour, are borne in spring, with a second flowering in late summer. This perennial's fleshy roots mean that it is very resistant to drought, and it seeds easily. It is a good colonising plant even in difficult areas. In gardens with moister soil it will form imposing clumps.

ORIGIN: Mediterranean
FLOWERING SEASON: April to June
HEIGHT: 0.7–1 m (26–38 in.)
SITUATION: sun
FROST-HARDY: ***
PROPAGATION: seed

Verbenaceae
Verbena bonariensis
(x 1.2)

A free-flowering verbena of erect growth with slender, branching stems, fine leaves, and flattened, luminous violet inflorescences. It brings an interesting note to summer flower-beds. Although short-lived, it seeds easily. It tolerates drought but prefers to be well watered in summer.

ORIGIN: South America
FLOWERING SEASON: July to October
HEIGHT: 1 m (38–40 in.)
SITUATION: sun
FROST-HARDY: **
PROPAGATION: seed

Violaceae
Viola sororia 'Freckles'
(x 5.9)

This violet has very pretty pale blue flowers blotched with purple, and pale green leaves. It forms strong clumps, and will seed itself in the rockery or border, or when used as underplanting.

FLOWERING SEASON: March to April
HEIGHT: 0.2 m (6–8 in.)
SITUATION: partial to full shade
FROST-HARDY: ***
PROPAGATION: division or seed

Growing perennials in the garden

Originating as they do in all parts of the world and every kind of natural environment, perennials can be grown in our gardens in many different ways. However, each plant should be offered the conditions that suit it best. It is up to the gardener to acquire some basic knowledge about the demands and aptitudes of various plants, and to assess the nature of the climate and soil of the garden in which they are to grow. The gardener is a budding agronomist and must find a judicious balance between three factors: the micro-climate, the soil, and the plant itself.

In general, perennials are grown together in three main ways: in a mixed border, in a rockery, or as ground cover or underplanting. However, they can also be grown with trees and shrubs, or in a wild garden or meadowland planting.

The mixed border

The idea of the mixed border was introduced into English gardens around the end of the nineteenth century, and has flourished ever since. A mixed border is a bed consisting chiefly of perennials, grown skilfully and harmoniously together to provide the eye with a long succession of flowers, and exploiting to the full the different heights, structures, shapes, and colours of the plants.

The bed itself may be straight or curved, depending on the design of the garden, and can be edged with a lawn or by a paved or gravel path. It may form an island, or a border down the side of a garden, or it can be of various other shapes. The idea is usually to make it look flexible and natural. Plants are arranged in groups or drifts, receding in order of height from low-growing edging plants such as alchemilla, heuchera, bergenia and geranium, through the centre of the bed, which is devoted to plants of medium height (such as helenium, coreopsis, liatris, campanula, scabious), to tall perennials (such as helianthus, miscanthus, kniphofia, macleaya) growing at the back, together with shrubs.

To be really successful, the mixed border should be planned from the start with a very clear concept in mind. Flowers will be the focal point. Since it is impossible to devise a flower-bed that is constantly in full bloom, it is a good idea to plan different areas to attract the eye with a succession of seasonal flowers.

If a visual balance is to be preserved, and if the foliage and outlines of all the perennials are to be seen to best effect, the mixed border needs regular maintenance (weeding, dead-heading, cutting back the more invasive plants). Observe these principles, and many plants will still look decorative even when they are not in bloom.

The rockery

The whole idea of a rockery derives from the natural environment. Typical features are the importance of its contours, the use of rocks or stones of different dimensions, and deliberate gaps left between the various plants.

People often decide to make a rockery out of part of the garden which seems naturally suitable, perhaps because it already contains some stony outcrops or a number of rocks. However, a bank can be specially laid out for the purpose, with blocks of stone placed in as natural a way as possible to create contours and overhanging ledges, and also to limit erosion. If there is no natural slope, the real rockery enthusiast will devise an entirely artificial creation which, with a little imagination, can be perfectly integrated with the rest of the garden. In fact on flat, moist ground it is often the only way to grow plants that naturally prefer a well-drained soil.

A rockery is the ideal way of cultivating plants that keep close to the ground, or are not vigorous and need a sloping perspective that the flower-bed cannot provide if they are to look their best. It will accommodate ground-cover plants that hug the natural contours or form cascades (iberis, dwarf campanulas, aubretia, sedums, helianthemum, *Artemisia schmidtiana* 'Nana', among others), cushion-forming plants (armerias, rockery pinks, house-leeks, saxifrages), and some erect plants (asphodel, sisyrinchium, grasses, and bulbs). The structure and texture of the plants are important factors, as is the harmony between their flowers. A good many of them have evergreen foliage, making the rockery one of the most reliably attractive features in the garden all the year round.

Ground cover

Planting ground cover enables you to colonise the entire surface area of the garden so that it is covered with attractive leaves and flowers almost throughout the year. While this is a useful and practical idea, it does not rule out the use of ground cover to achieve beautiful effects or the creation of unusual garden areas, either natural or sophisticated in appearance.

The principle of planting ground cover as a carpet of vegetation is to give each species its own space: how large that space is depends on the size of the garden. The contours should be elliptical or irregular, with planting in drifts to suggest a natural landscape. Alternatively, it can be interesting to mark different species off from each other by geometical lines in a mosaic pattern. Gardeners will opt for a natural or a more formal structure according to their own individual tastes.

Here are some of the many possibilities:

– On a bank: perennials can be used in many ways to cover a sloping surface completely. Suitable plants for this purpose include *Malvastrum lateritium, Geranium macrorrhizum, Phlox subulata, Phalaris arundinacea.* They will also help to retain the soil.

– As underplanting: gardeners are often anxious to find a way of covering the ground under the shade of trees or tall shrubs. There

are many shade-loving ground-cover plants with variegated, evergreen or deciduous leaves, some shiny like the foliage of the reliable periwinkle and pachysandra, some blotched or variegated, like *Aegopodium podagraria* 'Variegatum' and *Lamiastrum galeobdolon* 'Variegatum', while some are strikingly architectural like the leaves of acanthus. Many will form dense carpets, helping to create a delightful impression of natural undergrowth. They will combine easily with perennials that bear flowers on erect stems, for instance Japanese anemones or hostas.

– As a meadow: an open space planted with spreading herbaceous species, which are usually of an unsophisticated nature, that have a tendency to colonise the ground and can stand up to competition with each other. Such plants include centaurea, rudbeckia, oenothera, lychnis, kniphofia, gaura, gaillardia, Michaelmas daisy, achillea, lavatera and ornamental grasses (*Avena, Festuca, Pennisetum*). The gardener's work is reduced to a minimum in a meadow, and consists of cutting back the plants or mowing the area and removing unwanted weeds.

Perennials with other plants

It is unusual to design a garden consisting entirely of perennials. Usually the structural backbone of a garden will be shrubs and trees, with perennials added to introduce a note of colour, together with a good supply of flowers, and attractive foliage and plant structures.

Here are some possible ways of using perennials:

– In a foliage garden, where the main emphasis is on plants with striking, architectural, or vigorous leaves (*Fatsia japonica*, bamboos,

Musa basjoo – banana plant – *Arundo donax* 'Variegata', palms), grown with perennials with similar qualities (*Rheum palmatum, Melianthus major, Macleaya cordata, Arum aethiopicum*), tall grasses such as *Miscanthus*, and some perennials with bright flowers that will stand out well against the green background (canna, tall campanulas, agapanthus, and tall sages).

– In a traditional cottage garden of unpretentious design, which does not aim for landscaping effects and owes its charm to its spontaneity. Combining utility and beauty, the gardener will give preference to edible plants and herbs, with a few favourite ornamental plants such as roses, flowering shrubs, bulbs and annuals among them. Perennials have a place here too, particularly the more traditional species found in the gardens and flower arrangements of childhood memory. They can include ox-eye daisies, aquilegias, gaillardias, day lilies, and edging plants such as aubretia, small pinks, cerastium and alyssum.

– In a town garden where there is not much space, and the light is often cut off by nearby buildings and city trees, but the gardener still wants to create a pleasant outdoor area. Evergreen shrubs are particularly useful here, as are bamboos, grown in combination with such shade-tolerant perennials as pachysandras, lamium, alchemilla, aquilegia and *Euphorbia robbiae*.

– In a Mediterranean garden, which is typically dominated by evergreen foliage and the interplay of line, colour, and scent. Such a garden will contain many clipped or informal shrubs (rosemary, lavender, santolina, myrtle, box, bay, teucrium, cistus, pittosporum, ceanothus), and trees that carry a traditional symbolic significance, for instance cypress and olive. The flowers of perennials can add a touch of bright colour to such gardens, where they are particularly useful as ground cover (*Ceratostigma plumbaginoides, Erigeron karvinskianus, Sedum*) but may also include more erect, rustic plants such as *Gaura lindheimeri, Oenothera speciosa, Achillea filipendula, Salvia,* and *Euphorbia characias.*

– In a very dry, 'Californian' type of garden, where the bulk of the vegetation consists of sculptural plants and succulents (opuntia, yucca, agave, cordyline, *Chamaerops humilis*), shrubs for extremely dry conditions, and bulbs. The soil in such gardens is bare, or covered with gravel or other mineral substances. The lines are sharply drawn, the textures fleshy. Perennials are useful here to colonise empty spaces and add a note of colour with their flowers. Suitable species are *Delosperma cooperi, Convolvulus mauritanicus, Erigeron karvinskianus, Zauschneria californica,* and *Jacobinia suberecta.*

– In a container garden, where you may not be able to enjoy feeling the soil under your feet but you can still create a charming garden on a terrace, patio, or balcony. Combine evergreen shrubs such as box, euonymus, and pittosporum with some attractively architectural plants (palms, cordyline), and with annuals and perennials. It is important to choose species which will grow well in pots, and to provide them with suitable containers and the right growing medium. The most suitable perennials for such gardens have long flowering seasons and/or attractive foliage: plants such as bergenia, hosta, diascia, penstemon, periwinkle, the grasslike *Cyperus longus, Ceratostigma plumbaginoides, Oenothera speciosa, Convolvulus mauritanicus,* and *Erigeron karvinskianus.*

HOW TO CHOOSE PLANTS

A plant is very often bought because the gardener either already knew and liked it or fell in love with it at first sight. But the impulse buy, the seductive plant, may turn out to be inappropriate for the prevailing conditions of a particular garden. Growing perennials is not difficult if you observe a few basic principles. In choosing plants, it is useful to think about the ornamental qualities of each species, its aptitudes and requirements, and in general to understand your own garden.

Ornamental qualities

These qualities are not limited to the beauty and colour of the flowers. Every plant must be considered as a whole, with an eye to its integration in the garden landscape all the year round. You should take account of the time and length of its flowering season and the ornamental value of its foliage, the factor that lends the plant its appeal for the rest of the year. Think about the size and shape of the leaves, their colour, brilliance, any blotching or variegation, and whether they fall from the plant or remain on it in winter. You should also consider a plant's growth habit, height, and structure.

Demands and aptitudes

Whether perennials are native or exotic species, they all have their own natural habitats to which they are uniquely adapted. When they are introduced into a garden they should find conditions of soil type and climate that do not differ fundamentally from those of their natural environment. Each plant has

its own way of reacting to cold, wind, drought, or humidity, and makes its own demands on its situation (sun, partial shade, shade) and the nature of the soil (heavy, light, poor).

It is equally important to know how vigorous a perennial is, how much it will spread and whether it is a colonising plant. In fact the more vigorous a plant, the more likely it is to do well in conditions dissimilar to those of its original environment. Conversely, the more delicate it is, the more attentively the gardener should respect its preferences for certain kinds of soil or climate. In any case, a novice gardener is well advised to avoid difficult plants and choose stronger, adaptable species in order to build up the garden fast and efficiently. There will be time later, once more experience has been gained, to introduce into the garden more demanding species from very specific natural environments (such as *Meconopsis betonicifolia,* the blue Himalayan poppy, or the Californian poppy, *Romneya coulteri*).

Understanding the garden

A garden is a small universe in itself, seldom entirely uniform, and more often, as a result of the influence of nearby buildings, hedges, or old trees, consisting of a number of different micro-climates. Understanding its nature properly means studying the conditions of temperature, humidity, wind, sun, and the soil, taking one area after another. The gardener can then choose suitable plants on the basis of such observations. However, conditions may be improved by measures like soil improvement, the installation of an irrigation system, making a slope to drain water away, or planting a windbreak to provide additional shelter.

Temperature: even in a small garden the temperature is not exactly the same everywhere. Obviously frost will not be as hard at the foot of a south-facing wall as in the middle of a lawn. A little careful observation allows the gardener to discover what these differences of temperature are. The more protected areas can then be reserved for plants that are sensitive to colder conditions (diascia, zauschneria, delosperma, *Convolvulus mauritanicus*), while those which dislike heat, such as phlox, primrose and willow-herb, are best grown in the cooler parts of the garden. The effects of temperature cannot be isolated from other climatic factors such as wind and humidity. For instance, frost damage is increased by humidity in the air and by the sun, and too much heat will be even worse for plants in a windy situation that encourages fast drying out. A good understanding of the interplay of these factors is useful if you want to grow plants from climates that are hotter or colder than your own.

Covering plants in winter is a simple and effective way of protecting the rootstocks of certain tender species such as gunnera and melianthus. Dry leaves, straw, or horticultural fleece over the roots or around the plant will add several degrees of warmth. To avoid the risk of rotting, however, it is better not to cover the plant too early in the winter or leave it covered too long.

Humidity: although watering will help to counteract drought, increasingly acute conservation problems and the expense of managing this precious substance make it advisable to irrigate sensibly and sparingly. When watering, you should aim especially to compensate for dry periods in summer and concentrate on recently planted specimens. Apart from that, it is better to use sensible economic techniques such as choosing suitable plants, mulching between plants, and hoeing to eliminate weeds.

Wind: in some gardens in very exposed areas or by the sea, wind can exacerbate the effects of drought or frost damage and can cause windrock to plants. In such situations it is best to concentrate on sturdy, low-growing plants such as *Aster* x *dunosus* and low-growing *Dianthus*, plants with thick foliage such as phlomis and helianthemum, or species that are very supple and can bend to the wind without breaking, for instance ornamental grasses and catananche. Planting a windbreak of trees or shrubs can also have a beneficial effect on the climate in windy gardens.

Light: plants are often classified according to their need for sun, partial shade, or shade. In fact those simple terms cover a variety of situations, and call for a little further explanation.

Partial shade is present:
– in moderately sunny areas (two to four hours of sun a day);
– in open areas where there is no shade from plants, but no direct sun, for instance a north-facing wall.

Shade is present:
– under deciduous trees and shrubs, although there will be sun here in winter;
– under evergreen trees and shrubs: the shadiest of all situations.

There are subtle distinctions between various situations, and it is up to the gardener to assess them on the basis of experience.

Soil: in view of the many different possible kinds of terrain it would be risky to give precise directions for the best method of soil improvement. However, while the majority of perennials are happy in ordinary garden soil, some basic advice on common situations can be given. On heavy, easily compacted clay soil, dig in organic matter such as peat, humus or farmyard manure. On poor soil, the best supplements are organic fertilisers which will break down and release their minerals slowly and progressively into the soil, also improving its structure.

PLANTING

It is simple enough to add a few perennials to an existing bed or border: break up the soil to a depth of about 30 cm (12 in.), remove weeds, dig a hole, put the plant into the hole, and water it. If necessary a handful of organic fertiliser can be spread on the surface or mixed with the excavated soil.

When you have a whole new border, banks or rockery to plant, the entire surface needs careful preparation. To make future maintenance easier, it is best to eliminate all perennial weeds, either by digging them out, or chemically in the case of a really severe infestation with persistent plants like couch grass, bindweed, or brambles (use a glysophate-based non-residual* systemic herbicide). If soil improvement with garden compost or farmyard manure seems a good idea, spread it before turning over the soil to make sure it is well incorporated. Then dig the entire surface area with either a spade or a powered cultivator to a depth of about 30 cm (12 in.). If the area is a steep slope or a rockery, dig only the planting holes themselves.

After making these preparations it is a good idea to set out all the plants on the bed or border so that you can more easily assess the way you will use the space, trying to envisage the future effect. It is a good idea to plant each type in groups of three to five, at distances apart that will vary according to the ultimate size of each plant.

Once the plants are in, water them well. Depending on the climate and the time of year when you plant, you may have to water regularly over the first few weeks and even throughout the first year, particularly in the case of spring planting, to make sure that they will thrive in the future.

Planting time

Autumn (September to November) and early spring (February to April) are the best times to plant perennials. You should be able to conserve the amount of water used on them at these times. Planting from April to September will also give good results, particularly for late-flowering species, although a good deal of watering is necessary for plants put in during the summer. In a mild climate, autumn is the best planting time, while in a cold, wet climate the plants will grow away better in spring. As a general principle, do not plant frost-tender species until winter is over.

PROPAGATION

It is quite easy to increase your own stock of perennials, and plant propagation is both an interesting and a satisfying activity. There are several techniques, depending on the physiology of the plant.

From seed

Buying seed or harvesting it from your own plants is an easy way of propagating those species that will readily produce seed with a high germination rate and rapid growth. Such species include aquilegias, gaillardias, lupins, delphiniums, and echinaceas, as well as biennials such as foxgloves and hollyhocks. Sowing is generally from March to the summer. It should be done early for plants that can germinate, grow, and flower all in the same year, for instance *Centaurea montana*, *Gaura lindheimeri*, and *Coreopsis grandiflora*. Some seeds need special treatment in order to germinate, as for example the seeds of hellebores, which need to spend several weeks at a relatively cold temperature to break dormancy. Seed packets usually suggest any treatment that is advisable for germination.

For sowing in early spring, you need a sufficiently warm, sunny place such as a greenhouse, conservatory, or large window-sill. From April or May most seeds can be sown at outdoor temperatures.

The best and easiest method is to sow in a plastic or polystyrene seed tray, covering the seeds with compost to their own depth. The seed tray should remain moist but not wet, since seedlings easily rot. When the seedlings have two to six leaves (a few weeks after sowing) prick them out into small pots containing potting compost. Once the seedlings are big enough and have formed a good root system in the pots, plant them out in their final flowering positions in the garden.

Growing from seed is a simple method, but cannot be used to propagate a certain number of cultivars with seeds that do not

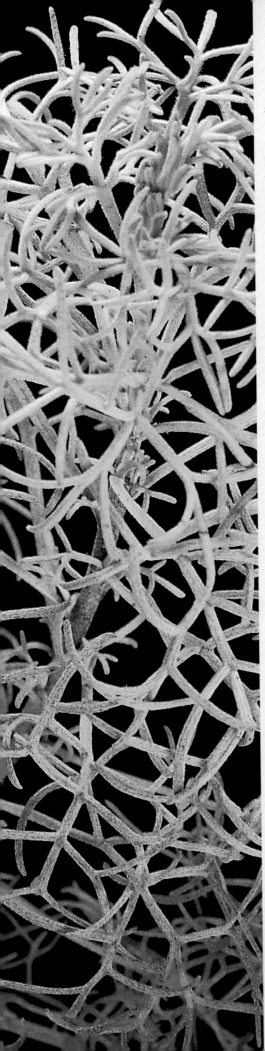

always produce plants identical with their parent. For this reason, it is often a more interesting prospect for experienced gardeners to use vegetative means of propagation (cuttings, suckers, runners, or stolons* and root division), which will give you young plants ready to be planted out sooner.

Division

Division of the rootstock is an easy way of increasing clump-forming perennials such as the Michaelmas daisy, achillea, solidago, hemerocallis, hostas, and ornamental grasses. Division is best carried out in spring, at the start of the growing season, or in autumn for spring-flowering species. Dig up the plant with a spade, cut back the stems and shorten the roots. Then divide the rootstock into as many pieces as there are crowns with attached roots in the clump. The more robust species can be replanted at once; more delicate species will grow away better if they are raised in a pot or other container for a while, until they have formed a good root system (species like this include diascia, *Campanula carpatica*, and *Artemisia schmidtiana* 'Nana').

The same technique can be used for rhizomatous plants, which include Solomon's seal and iris, tuberous plants such as peony and dicentra, and bulbous plants such as crocosmia. Each separate piece of a rhizome, tuberous root, or bulb can then be used as a potential new plant.

Suckers and runners

Suckers are lateral shoots from the rootstock; they form underground and come to the surface to produce new stems. They then grow roots from their underground parts, and can easily be lifted and separated from the parent plant. Species propagated in this way include tradescantia and physalis.

Runners or stolons are supple stems which naturally bend down to the surface of the soil and root once in contact with it. The most familiar example is the strawberry. Individual plantlets or offshoots develop, and can be separated from the parent. Other examples include lamium and periwinkle. To speed up rooting, encourage the runners to come into contact with the soil.

Like pieces of divided rootstock, the separated plantlets can be either planted directly in their new positions or grown on in pots until large enough to plant out.

Cuttings

A cutting is a section of stem that has been placed in a humid environment in order to encourage it to put out adventitious roots and form a new plantlet. This is a delicate technique, for the cutting must be carefully kept alive until the new roots can feed it themselves. The method is especially useful for woody plants: trees, shrubs, and sub-shrubs. However, it is also recommended for some perennials that are difficult or impossible to propagate by most other methods, including sub-shrubby species like helianthemum and penstemon, and fleshy plants like sedums.

The same technique is used when offshoots or runners which have not yet grown roots are taken from a plant, as with houseleeks, saxifrages, *Phlox subulata*, lamiums and periwinkles.

It is a good idea to use hormone rooting powder to encourage the cuttings of the more difficult, sub-shrubby species such as penstemons to form roots.

BUYING PERENNIALS

Today it is an increasingly easy option for gardeners who like perennials to buy many of their favourite species from specialist nurseries. They are raised in pots or containers with a capacity of 1, 2, or even 3 litres (2, 4 or 6 pints). Only a few species, such as peonies and hostas, are sometimes sold bare-rooted. Perennials in small pots can be bought for planting out from September to March; later, the 2-litre (4 pint) size of container is to be preferred, since the plant will then have a better-developed root system, enabling it to grow away more easily. When buying, you should pay more attention to the condition of the roots and the strength and health of the plant than to the amount of foliage or number of flower-buds on it. Its potential is the crucial point.

It is better to buy plants that have been raised or hardened off out of doors. A greenhouse-grown perennial which has put out leaves too soon because of the protected environment may suffer from shock when it is suddenly planted outside, and its future development could be affected. Make sure the plants are properly labelled, particularly if they are not in flower. In any case, the flowering period is not usually the best time to buy, except when a species has a number of different cultivars, and so you can avoid a possible unwelcome surprise later by buying a plant in flower. If you cannot put the plants in at once, keep them in a sheltered spot and water them regularly.

THE DEVELOPMENT OF THE GARDEN

So now you have thought about the garden, planned, prepared, and planted it. Time for a well-earned rest … or is it? Not exactly: planting a garden has made you a gardener, and the story continues. Above and beyond general maintenance – such as weeding, pruning, hoeing – the constant development of the garden can be fascinating.

If it is a new garden, laid out around a new house, it will develop very quickly. During the first few years the perennials will always be the most conspicuous plants, rapidly producing a visual effect once they are in the ground. Then the trees and shrubs will become established, and with them the structure of the whole garden will become obvious. Spaces fill up; areas of sun and shade change. Some perennials may find they have to compete for space and light.

The same phenomenon occurs in an older garden 'renovated' by the addition of new perennials. It is unusual for Nature to respect a plan exactly as it was first designed. Individual species do not necessarily fill the space intended for them. They may spread too much, or on the contrary they may suffer from competition with neighbouring plants. One approach is to try forcing rebellious plants to respect your wishes. If you take this line then you must take action, but do observe the garden and think carefully first. Most perennials will tolerate and even thrive on transplantation. If a species will not adapt to the situation where you planted it, why not put it somewhere that suits it better? If a plant threatens to take over the entire bed or border, transplant it to an area where you can appreciate its vigour.

The other approach is to let Nature do as it likes. The more a plant is inclined to make suckers or runners, the more difficult it will be to stop it spreading. It is advisable to plant it together with equally vigorous species, or with shrubs. But it would be a pity to think of its good health as a fault; it is up to the gardener to take advantage of that quality, for instance by dividing the rootstock to provide new plants for other parts of the garden. *Rudbeckia fulgida*, for instance, a very attractive plant with its late flowering season, is ideal, and never boring when planted to add drifts of bright colour. Achilleas, coreopsis, solidago, heleniums, and *Oenothera speciosa* can be used in the same way.

A number of species, moreover, will spontaneously increase themselves. They disperse their seeds to other parts of the garden, where they will often grow to very good effect. Such self-willed species as gaura, centaurea, *Oenothera speciosa*, and some biennials or short-lived perennials like clary sage, foxglove, and hollyhock can be allowed to have their own way.

Self-seeding can be a very useful way of populating some areas which resist any other efforts to plant them up. If you have walls or flights of old stone steps in the garden, for instance, it is ideal to plant valerian, *Erigeron karvinskianus* or wallflower, near them. The seeds of these plants will lodge and germinate in the tiniest cracks.

It can also be useful to keep certain wild plants that appear of their own accord and often look very pretty: fennel, mullein, wild arums, small veronicas and so on. Others, however – nightshade and goosefoot spring to mind – should be eliminated without mercy; they produce a huge number of seeds that remain capable of germination over several years.

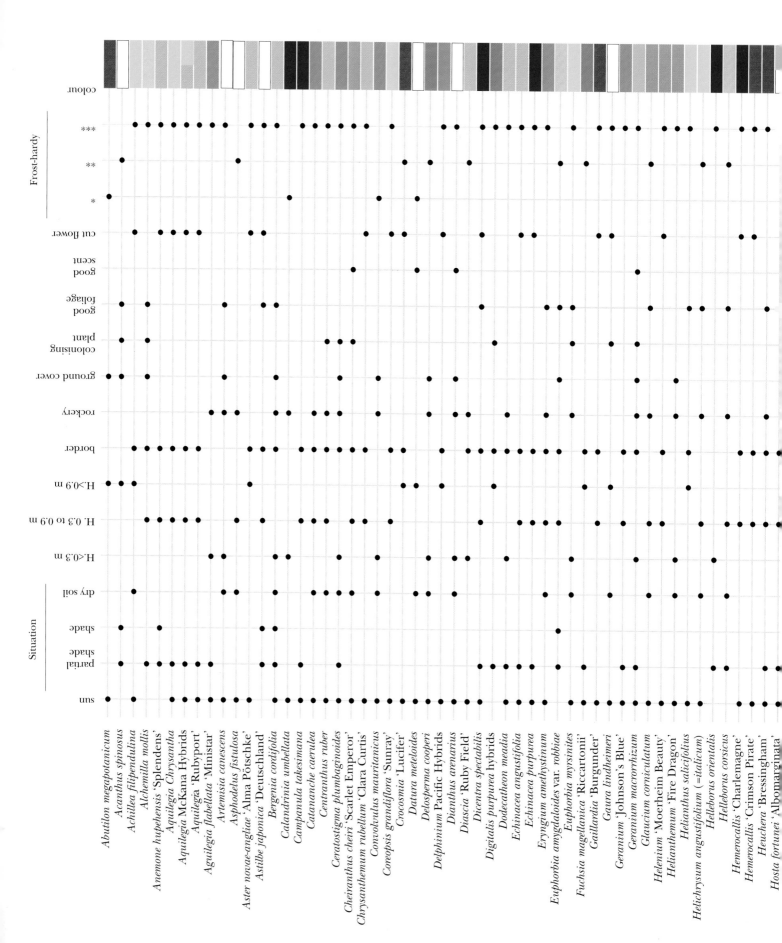

Houttuynia cordata 'Chameleon'
Jaborosa integrifolia
Jacobinia suberecta
Kniphofia hybrids
Lavatera thuringiaca
Liatris spicata
Lobelia laxiflora
Lupinus Russell hybrids
Macleaya cordata
Malva sylvestris ssp. mauritiana
Malvastrum lateritium
Marrubium cylleneum
Melianthus major
Mimulus aurantiacus
Miscanthus sacchariflorus
Morina longifolia
Nepeta mussinii
Nicotiana sylvestris
Oenothera speciosa
Ophiopogon japonicus
Origanum tournefortii
Paeonia lactiflora 'Sarah Bernhardt'
Penstemon 'Souvenir d'Adrien Régnier'
Phlomis russeliana
Phlomis tuberosa
Phlox paniculata
Phygelius capensis
Physalis franchetii
Platycodon grandiflorus
Polygonatum odoratum
Pulsatilla vulgaris 'Rubra'
Ratabida columnaris f. pulcherrima
Rheum palmatum 'Atrosanguineum'
Romneya coulteri
Salvia argentea
Salvia rutilans
Salvia sclarea
Salvia uliginosa
Saxifraga Aureopunctata
Saxifraga x arendsii
Scabiosa caucasica
Schizostylis coccinea 'Major'
Sedum kamtschaticum 'Variegatum'
Sisyrinchium angustifolium
Solanum mauritianum
Stachys byzantina
Stokesia laevis
Tanacetum densum ssp. amanii
Tradescantia × andersonia 'Karminglut'
Trollius chinensis 'Golden Queen'
Verbena bonariensis
Vinca major 'Variegata'
Viola sororia 'Freckles'
Zauschneria californica

Glossary

Angiosperm: the sub-section of the plant kingdom consisting of flowering plants that produce seeds enclosed in a fruit.

Annual: term for a plant that completes its entire cycle of development, from germination to death, within the same year. Some plants that are annuals in European climates may be perennials in their original environments.

Biennial: term for plants completing their cycle of development in two years. They germinate and grow in the first year; in the second year they flower and set seed before dying.

Capitulum: an inflorescence that appears to be a single flower, but really consisting of a large number of stemless florets crammed close together.

Colloid: a substance consisting of tiny particles (liquids or solids) suspended in a liquid.

Corymb: a flat-topped or domed inflorescence consisting of a number of florets with stems of different lengths alternating on the main stem.

Deciduous: a term applied to any part of a plant (most usually the leaves) that dies back at the end of the growing season.

Dicotyledon: a term for a plant with seeds that contain one embryo plantlet that emerges with two cotyledons (embryonic seed leaves).

Evergreen: a plant with foliage that persists throughout the year.

Hardy: the term for a plant that can survive difficult conditions (too much water, drought or cold), although it is most commonly used for resistance to cold conditions, or frost-hardiness.

Herbaceous: the term for a plant that does not form a rigid woody stem but consists of soft vegetation, dying down in the autumn and coming up again the following spring.

Mixed border: a border consisting mainly of mixed perennials, with different flowering seasons, planted to give a variety of size, shape and colour.

Non-residual: said of a substance that disperses after acting. A non-residual herbicide will not remain in the soil, and does not pollute the environment.

Osmosis: the progress of a solvent (in this case water) through a membrane from a diluted to a concentrated solution, with a tendency to produce the same concentration in each part of the membrane.

Rhizomatous: term for a plant with a rhizome, or creeping underground stem, usually swollen and fleshy.

Runner, stolon: a creeping stem, usually above the ground, which produces new plantlets that will easily root when separated from the parent plant.

Semi-evergreen: foliage is semi-evergreen when it remains on the plant all the year round except in very severe winters, when it will drop.

Sucker: a new stem thrown up from the creeping underground root of a plant. Suckers can be separated from the parent plant and will easily root themselves.

Supercooled: said of a liquid which in some conditions still remains liquid below its normal freezing point. Water is supercooled if it is still liquid below a temperature of 0° C (32° F).

Tuberous: term for a plant with an underground storage organ (a root tuber or less frequently a stem tuber) which is thickened at one end.

Umbelliferous: a description for plants with an inflorescence in which the stems of the florets originate at the same point, reaching the same height as they separate from one another and forming a kind of umbrella shape.

Index

Page numbers refer to text or captions, except those in italics, which indicate illustrations.

Abutilon megapotamicum, 50
Acanthaceae, 86, 88
Acanthus spinosus, 86, *87*
Achillea 'Lachsschönheit', *13*
Achillea filipendulina, 18, 118
Aegopodium podagraria 'Variegatum', 117
Aizoaceae, 88
Alchemilla mollis, 110
Alstroemeria aurantiaca, 15
Amaryllidaceae, *15*
Anemone hupehensis 'Splendens', *64, 65*
Apiaceae, *5*
Apocynaceae, 90
Aquilegia 'Chrysantha', *62, 63*
Aquilegia flabellata 'Ministar', *66, 67*
Aquilegia vulgaris 'Nora Barlow', *66*
Artemisia cansescens, 18, 19
Artemisia 'Powis Castle', *9*
Artemisia schmidtiana 'Nana', 117, *122*
Arum aethiopicum, 118
Arundo donax 'Variegata', 118
Asphodelus fistulosa, 11
Aster novae-angliae 'Alma Pötschke', 20, *21*
Aster x *dumosus,* 120
Asteraceae, 5, *13, 16–31*
Astilbe japonica 'Deutschland', *76, 77*
Bergenia cordifolia, 77
Brassicaceae, *12*
Calandrinia umbellata, 108
Campanula takesimana, 90, 91
Campanulaceae, 90–93
Caryophyllaceae, 9
Catananche caerulea, 20
Ceanothus, 118
Centaurea montana, 7, *121*
Centranthus ruber, 114
Ceratostigmatus plumbaginoides, 22,
106–107, 108, 118, 119
Chamaerops humilis, 118
Cheiranthus cheiri 'Scarlet Emperor', *12*
Chrysanthemum rubellum 'Clara Curtis', *22*
Cistaceae, *94, 95*
Commelinaceae, 94
Convolvulaceae, *93*
Convolvulus mauritanicus, 93, 119
Coreopsis grandiflora, 121
Coreopsis verticillata, 22

Crassulaceae, 96
Crocosmia 'Lucifer', *102*
Cyperus longus, 119
Datura meteloides, 82
Delosperma cooperi, 88, 119
Delphinium Pacific Hybrids, *68*
Dianthus arenarius, 9, 120
Diascia 'Ruby Field', *14*
Dicentra spectabilis, 54–55, 56
Digitalis purpurea , 7
Dipsaceae, *6,* 96, *97*
Dodecatheon meadia, 108, 109
Echinacea angustifolia, 22, *23*
Echinacea purpurea, 24, 25
Erigeron karvinskianus, 118, 119, *123*
Eryngium amethystinum, 5
Euphorbia amygdaloides var. *robbiae, 98,*
118
Euphorbia characias, 118
Euphorbia myrsinites, 98, 99
Euphorbiaceae, *98, 99*
Fabaceae, *100*
Fatsia japonica, 118
Fuchsia magellanica 'Riccartonii', 58, *59*
Gaillardia 'Burgunder', *26*
Gaura lindheimeri, 60, 118, 121
Geraniaceae, 100, *101*
Geranium 'Johnson's Blue', *100*
Geranium macrorrhizum, 100, *101,* 117
Geum chiloense, 9
Glaucium corniculatum, 52, 53
Helenium 'Moerheim Beauty', 26, *27*
Helianthemum 'Fire Dragon', *94, 95*
Helianthus salicifolius, 28
Helichrysum italicum (*angustifolium*),
28, 29
Helleborus argutifolius (*corsicus*), *70*
Hemerocallis 'Charlemagne', *42, 43*
Hemerocallis 'Crimson Pirate', *44*
Heuchera 'Bressingham', *7, 78*
Hosta fortunei 'Albomarginata', *45*
Houttuynia cordata 'Chameleon', *111*
Iridaceae, 102–105
Jaborosa integrifolia, 82
Jacobinia suberecta, 88, 119
Kniphofia hybrids, *46*
Lamiaceae, 5, *32–41*

Lamiastrum galeobdolon 'Variegatum',
9, 117
Lavandula angustifolia, 7
Lavatera thuringiaca, 50, 51
Liatris spicata, 29
Liliaceae, 5, *11, 42–47*
Lobelia laxiflora, 92, 93
Lupinus Russell hybrids, *100*
Macleaya cordata, 9, 56, 118
Malva sylvestris ssp. *mauritiana,* 48, *49*
Malvaceae, 5, *48–51*
Malvastrum lateritium, 117
Marrubium cylleneum, 34
Meconopsis betonicifolia, 119
Melianthaceae, 105
Melianthus major, 105
Mimulus aurantiacus, 8
Miscanthus saccarifolius, 105
Miscanthus sinensis, 9
Morina longifolia, 96, 97
Nepeta mussinii, 34, 35
Nicotiana sylvestris, 80, 81
Oenothera speciosa, 60, 118, 119, *123*
Oenotheraceae, 5, *58–61*
Ophiopogon japonicus, 46, 47
Origanum tournefortii, 37
Paeonis lactiflora 'Sarah Bernhardt', 7,
70, 71
Papaveraceae, 5, *52–57*
Penstemon 'Souvenir d'Adrien Régnier',
112, *113*
Phalaris arundinaceae, 117
Phlomis russeliana, 36, 37
Phlomis tuberosa, 38
Phlox douglasii, 7
Phlox paniculata, 10
Phlox subulata, 117, *122*
Phygelius capensis, 9, 112
Physalis franchetti, 84, 85
Platycodon grandiflorus, 93
Plumbaginaceae, *106–109*
Poaceae, *105*
Polemoniaceae, *10*
Polygonatum odoratum, 46
Portulaceae, *108*
Primulaceae, 108, *109*
Pulsatilla vulgaris 'Rubra', *7, 72*

Ranunculaceae, 5, *62–73*
Ratabida columnaris f. *pulcherrima, 17*
Rheum palmatum, 118
Romneya coulteri, 56, 57, 119
Rosaceae, 110
Rudbeckia fulgida, 123
Salvia argentea, 38
Salvia rutilans, 40
Salvia sclarea, 38, 39
Salvia uliginosa, 9, 40, 41
Saururaceae, *111*
Saxifraga aizoon 'Minor', *7*
Saxifraga x *arendsii, 79*
Saxifraga x *urbium* 'Aureopunctata',
74, 75
Saxifragaceae, 5, *74–79*
Scabiosa caucasica, 6
Schizostylis coccinea 'Major', *103*
Scrophulariaceae, *7, 8, 14, 112, 113*
Sedum kamtschaticum 'Variegatum', *96*
Sisyrinchium angustifolium, 104, 105
Solanaceae, 5, *80–85*
Solanum mauritianum, 84
Stachys byzantina, 32, 33
Stokesia laevis, 30
Tanacetum densum ssp. *amanii, 31*
Tradescantia x *andersonia* 'Karminglut',
94
Trollius chinensis 'Golden Queen', *72, 73*
Valerianaceae, *114*
Verbena bonariensis, 7, 9, 114
Verbenaceae, *114*
Vinca major 'Variegata', *90*
Viola sororia 'Freckles', *114, 115*
Violaceae, *114, 115*
Zauschneria californica, 60, 61, 119

Bibliography

Roger Phillips and Martyn Rix, *Perennials*, 2 vols., Pan Books, 1991.

Leo Jelitto and Wilhelm Schacht, transl. Michael E. Epp, *Hardy Herbaceous Perennials*, Batsford, 1990.

Richard Hansen and Friedrich Stahl, *Perennials and their Garden Habitats*, transl. Richard Ward, Cambridge University Press, 1993.

Penelope Hobhouse, *Plants in Garden History*, Pavilion Books, 1992.

Marina Schinz with Susan Littlefield, *Visions of Paradise: Themes and Variations on the Garden*, Thames & Hudson, 1985.

Marguerite Duval, *The King's Garden*, transl. Annette Tomaken and Claudine Cowan, University Press of Virginia, 1982.

The Royal Horticultural Society Gardeners' Encyclopedia of Plants and Flowers, ed. Christopher Brickell, Dorling Kindersley, 1989, rev. 1994.

Useful addresses

THE ROYAL HORTICULTURAL SOCIETY
80 Vincent Square, London SW1P 2PE

THE ROYAL BOTANIC GARDENS
Kew, near Richmond, Surrey.

THE ROYAL BOTANIC GARDEN
Edinburgh.

CAMBRIDGE UNIVERSITY BOTANIC GARDEN
Brookside, Cambridge.

OXFORD UNIVERSITY BOTANIC GARDEN
Oxford.

Some nurseries

Pépinière du Mas de Quinty, 30 440 Roquedur.
Nursery of the author, where all the pictures in the book have been taken.

Bressingham Gardens, Diss, Norfolk.

Beth Chatto Gardens, Elmstead Market, Colchester, Essex.

Notcutts, Ipswich Road, Woodbridge, Suffolk, IP12 4AF.

Scotts Nurseries, Merriott, Somerset, TA16 5PL.